This is a treat... Penny Billington shows us how to make deeper contact with and to befriend the energetic forms of trees in a refreshingly down-to-earth way, in a series of nine charms... The book's appeal is not limited by any particular belief system or by the need for any prior knowledge. Wherever the reader might be, all they need to begin is the will to reach out in respect and friendship to another form of life, and time.—former Librarian, Society of the Inner Light

Nine Ways to Charm a Dryad is a Druid's dream, gently guiding you on a path to deepen your relationship with the spirits of trees with lyrical meditations and provocative questions that get you thinking in new ways about what it means to be in relationship with the trees...A book for the curious, for the tree-lover, and for the Druid in all of us!—Philip Carr-Gomm, author of *Druid-Craft*

In a time when so many people are disconnected and weary, Billington's work is a breath of fresh air. *Nine Ways to Charm a Dryad* is a complete course in how to speak and interact with the spirits of nature, working with them to achieve inner and outer transformation. Her work encourages us to connect with the trees through mind, body, and spirit through clear instructions, rituals, and activities—and through this work, reconnect with the living earth. For those seeking transformation and a meaningful connection with nature, this work is for you!—Dana O'Driscoll, grand archdruid of the Ancient Order of Druids in America and author of *Sacred Actions: Living the Wheel of the Year Through Earth-Centered Sustainable Practices*, *Tarot of Trees*, and *Plant Spirit Oracle*

Nine Ways
to Charm
a Dryad

Penny Billington is a Druid teacher, speaker, and author. She is an active member of the Order of Bards, Ovates and Druids and has edited the order's magazine, *Touchstone*, for nineteen years; she is also a graduate of the Annwn Foundation. She regularly facilitates workshops in the UK and Europe, organises rituals, gives lectures, and runs a Druid Grove. She is also a frequent guest on the order's Facebook group events "Tea with a Druid" and "The Private Magician's Club." Exploring and studying Druidry, which she blends with aspects of the Western Mystery Tradition, keeps her personal practice fluid, fresh, and alive to mystery. Penny is also the author of a Druid detective series. She lives on the green Somerset levels near Glastonbury, England.

A Magical Adventure
to Connect with the
Spirit of Trees

Penny Billington

NINE WAYS TO CHARM

A DRYAD

LLEWELLYN
PUBLICATIONS

FIRST EDITION
First Printing, 2022

Cover design by Shannon McKuhen
Cover and interior art by Meraylah Allwood
Interior design by Rebecca Zins

Llewellyn Publications is a registered
trademark of Llewellyn Worldwide Ltd.

Library of Congress Cataloging-in-Publication Data
Pending

ISBN 978-0-7387-6875-5

Llewellyn Publications
A Division of Llewellyn Worldwide Ltd.
2143 Wooddale Drive
Woodbury, MN 55125-2989
www.llewellyn.com

 Printed in the United States of America

For the three realms,

the many worlds,

and the deep green dreaming of the trees.

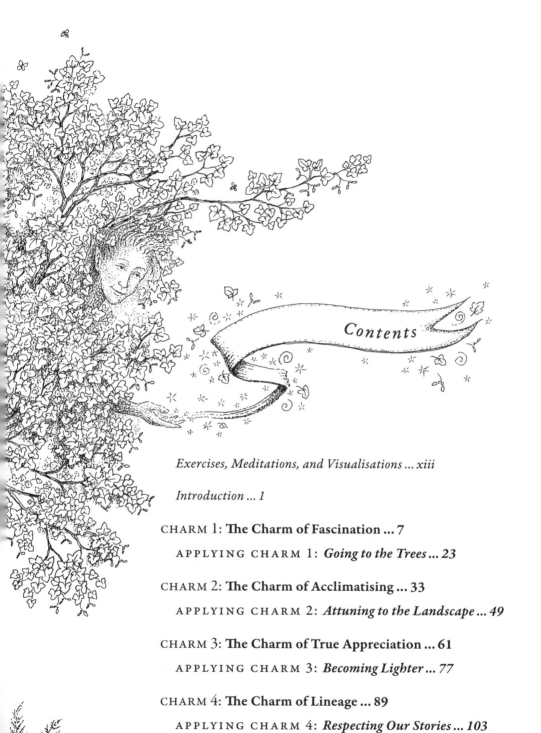

Contents

Exercises, Meditations, and Visualisations

Introduction

Welcome to a magical adventure—a new way of understanding the world through nature. It's the way we related to it as children, when all life seemed inspirited and the landscape fed our imaginations. Our sentient earth lives and breathes. It supports myriad forms of life, all with their own intelligence, and of them, our most accessible teachers, supporters, and healers are the trees and their dryads.

This book aims to guide you in building a relationship with a dryad. We'll call this process charming, for "charm" means to act magically, and the dryads can bring us enchantment; and because it is by being charming that we make friends. If humans are our only friends, we might, although happy, have sensed that life has more to offer. I believe that it does and that now is the time to expand out into the world of nature.

The nine themed charms include meditative exercises and many ideas for writing, artwork, and ways of communicating with nature. Every charm is followed by a more active section—"applying the charm"—where we take those ideas out to a tree. Alternative suggestions are included if you have health, age, or mobility restrictions. I'm delighted that three colleagues, speaking from personal experience, have contributed to appendix 5, which is specifically for readers in these situations. The natural world loves inclusivity and diversity, and each of us is an integral, vital part of it. The work we do will benefit both us and beleaguered nature.

Each of the nine charms describes a different way of approaching our dryad association to help us gradually to build our relationship. If you love your cat, dog, or other companion animal—if "pet" does not properly hon-our your friendship—then you have been practicing interspecies commu-nication for years. You will know just how freeing and relaxing this can be compared to human exchanges.

But who are the dryads, and how can we learn from them? Ancient stories say a dryad is a nymph or spirit living within a tree, and its life depends upon it; for a fuller description of the classical definition, see page 267. For us, the dryad represents the spirit of the tree: one that is gracious, long-lived, and full of life force. The numinous quality of "spirit" defies firm definition so we can view dryads in a variety of ways, for the image is just the tool to help our communication. We may imagine a dryad as a potent life force indivisi-ble from the tree's physicality; as a roving tree nymph or a vegetative entity; as female, male, transgender, hermaphroditic, humanoid, or other form. For you, a dryad might be able to leave its tree for short times or be a walking tree with its face delineated in the trunk, beloved of Victorian illustrators. Over the course of the book, we can use all these interpretations. It is the accep-tance of the tree spirit that will be constant.

When we are cut off from nature, we feel that something important is missing; we feel dissatisfied and incomplete. Not recognizing the cause, we try to satisfy the lack. The irony is that what we try often takes us further and further from the forest—from the earth, our home. By actively seeking and seeing wonder in the natural world, we can re-enter the wood whose trees converse—the forests of the world that still whisper their magic to us.

The spirits of the trees are active in our children's books. Within their pages Ratty still hears the song of the wind in the willows, beech and birch maidens live on in Narnia, and on Prince Edward Island, Anne of Green Gables still dreams of them. Our wistful feelings are a dim recollection that we accepted unconditionally as children: that there are spirits in trees with whom we can communicate. We fear we have lost that capacity, but the stir-ring that moved your hand toward this book tells you that it is just waiting to reawaken. We are responding to the call of the dryads, who are whispering that, although long-neglected, our ability to connect with the trees is still within us. And if we choose to listen—and act—then our world can expand amazingly.

To prove, this minute, the connection is still there, pick a memory of a beautiful landscape, drinking wine watching the sunset, listening to the sea, or smelling heather on a moorland. If you remember and sit with that memory, it will reactivate the refreshment you experienced; no matter how or where you are now, you will feel that calm joy through remembering a precious connection with nature. And it happens every time we let the subtle influence of the living landscape in, both in the present and through memory.

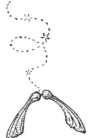

*Being happily in nature is
what makes us feel relaxed.
Being relaxed is when we
are most alive to spirit.*

Those memories are still clear because they were when we paused—took a last look, an extra deep breath, fixed it in memory. We were aware of being content in the moment and not at the mercy of future or past. Our appreciation was all the thanks that nature needed. And these feelings of being in tune with nature, when all is well with our world, can be a part of our everyday lives, spontaneously occurring, if only we allow time. How wonderful to expect that feeling habitually! How wonderful if a local dryad would help us to access it! We can start to develop internal resources to encourage this way of relating to the world. It is the start of living a life of enchantment.

Most of us grow up thinking that true magic is for children's books or is a craft needing much discipline and study and that magicians are set apart. That is one approach. But mine is a natural magic, and I believe that most people do not want to "do" magic but live magically, and for that, a simple, regular routine of tree connection can be transformative.

Worldwide, from huge lush rain forests to stunted desert trees, from dense woodland to sparse copse, our tree cousins are growing patiently all around.

In our city streets, backyards, parks, and wild spaces, they are just waiting to communicate their friendship and support. We have free movement; we have voices; we have a consciousness. All these things tell us that it is our job to make the first move. We need to approach and ask in a way that will gain goodwill and tempt the shy spirit of a tree to communicate with us for our mutual benefit. I call this "charming your dryad," and I hope the guidelines in the book, from initial contact to growing a relationship, will result in a trusted friendship for you.

When you begin to make a relationship, it will be a mutual choice between you and a tree spirit. From its point of view, you will be the dryad's human friend. It is hard not to come from a human-centric viewpoint, so this reminder of the awareness of the living world is sprinkled through the book. To communicate, we need to believe in the understanding, intelligence, and empathy of the trees, or sentience; it is the first understanding in this work. Accepting it as a working premise, then all we need to do is awaken the skills we have learnt from babyhood. Starting is that simple.

Accepting that communion is two-way, we will contrive ways of noticing and interpreting the dryad's responses and the parameters of our relationship. That does take time and commitment, but I hope it will be fueled by your inner fascination for that wonderful tree person who is long-lived, wise, and totally in touch with the seasons. I believe that the regular and immediate results you may achieve will encourage you to continue.

Historically, humankind has always understood that trees are a close neighbour-species, as evidenced by stories from every culture worldwide. We feel that our lives are bound together. They are our kin, with their trunks and limbs and crown—all words we use to describe parts of our own bodies. Their "feet" may be rooted, but we also feel gravity, which roots us to earth, and many of us are searching for our roots. Tree people have always been seen as very similar to us: the spirits of the trees help characters from fairy tales and shelter deserted children; they trap wicked goblins and give gifts to the pure; they lend their strength to deserving people and confound the wicked.

Trees can draw, mesmerise, bewitch, enchant, and frighten us. They have personalities; and in groves, copses, woods, and forests, they create a formidable atmosphere. Visiting at twilight, we remember Tolkien's forests of Middle Earth, "full of secret purpose"; Red Riding Hood's forest, where the only safety is sticking to the path; the forest where we might chance upon dwarves, goblins, and Rumpelstiltskin; and the Forbidden Forest of Hogwarts School of Witchcraft and Wizardry. Like walking into a party full of strangers, we can feel challenged, awed, and ill at ease, an atavistic feeling that we must respect, yet these are places of transformation. Best, then, to pick our times carefully, to go gently, having a dryad friend, having learnt some communication skills, and especially having learnt to listen.

I would love for you to read, wander, sink into original thought, make notes in the book's margins, underline anything that captures your imagination, and stuff the book into your pocket to flick through whenever you have a spare five minutes or consult when you go for a walk. If you embrace its message, it will soon be dog-eared and well-thumbed. It may become your passport to a life of wonder...

We are driven by a longing to experience the world truly and intimately as our home. We are ready to take our rightful place and feel that a generous dryad spirit is just waiting to mentor us.

We are ready to start charming our dryad. Welcome to the adventure!

Q: Why would we wish to charm a dryad? *A:* Because we long for re-enchantment.

Charm 1

THE CHARM OF

FASCINATION

*B*reathe deeply. Hush. Turn the corner and step between two young oaks.

A branch moves; leaves rustle. An acorn bounces on the packed path. Listen to the green silence: listen. Breathe in the dew-drenched forest perfume: breathe. Soft air caresses you: feel. Allow yourself to pass into forest time. Become spellbound.

Your eyes adjust to woodland-sight,
to the green shadows and sun's rays.

The wood holds its breath; then,
with a sigh, the trees move with a
sinuous, fluid magic. It is as if bark
covers long limbs, stretching after the
winter hibernation. Boughs beckon,
and the birds are a choir. Move
through a cathedral of living columns,
toward a distant tree...

A squirrel chatters: an acorn falls,
and a sudden wind tears at twigs.

The moment has gone; the trees
resume their normal appearance,
but now you have an inkling of their
sentience.

Resume your walk...

WE HAVE AN inclination to start walking… What might the forest reveal? Sentience is the ability to feel. Intuition is the ability to understand instinctively: beyond rational thought, at a deep level, we *know*.

> *Our intuitive understanding*
> *that trees are sentient and that*
> *we can communicate with them*
> *is the bedrock of this book.*

Take a moment to remember when you might have had this sense of the noticing intelligence of nature. If you can't think of an instance, no worries. You will soon have a full memory! You might like to copy out the question and answer at the top of this charm on the first page of your journal, then write down any feelings of sentience as you remember them. This will be the start of your charmer's journal.

We use the words "charm" and "charming" routinely. Now we will use it with awareness and feeling in order to reclaim its potency. It is a key to the start of a magical adventure as we explore the realm of the nature spirits.

To *charm* means

✻ to delight greatly

✻ to use one's ability to attract in order to influence

✻ to control or achieve as if by magic

These three are inextricably linked, for delight, pleasure, attraction, and magic are all relational. How do they apply to us as personalities?

We start by asking:

> ❦ Do we delight others of our own species?
>
> ❦ Do we find others delightful?
>
> ❦ Do we please and attract?
>
> ❦ Do we feel we are a bit magical?
>
> ❦ Do others agree?

The qualities of delight and attraction will help us to charm our dryad. Not many of us have tried to develop this part of ourselves consciously, but now we will begin to focus on delight and being delightful.

You might wonder if we will "do" charms—as in spells or potions. That will not be our focus, and what we do will depend on the human-dryad relationship that develops. It's a question of temperament and inclination. Charming is rooted in an intangible quality of communication that we develop individually, so proscriptive scripts and spells would be counter-productive. Rest assured that, even without specific spells, in charming your dryad you will be performing natural magic. Within this book you will find many pointers and guidelines to help you.

So, to achieve the charm of fascination, we'll start gently to transform into the sort of people who charm, who have charisma. That relies on your enthusiastic agreement, so make a promise to yourself now that you'll commit to it. Who doesn't want to add to their charisma?

Charm and charisma are entwined. Charismatic people charm us with their self-confidence, focus, and empathy. They seem to have a stable inner purpose but are also directed outward, deeply interested in the world and other people rather than concentrating on themselves. These shining people genuinely have time for us; they find us engrossing, and we love them for it. We are charmed in their presence. Does that describe you yet? Is that how you would like to be?

No one can promise us charisma, but working through the exercises with commitment will focus us; developing a relationship with the trees and our dryad will encourage looking outward and give us a new perspective. Having a nature connection takes the pressure off our obsession with human relationships and makes them more harmonious. An outlook underpinned by a nature connection increases joy. It makes us genuinely fascinated as part of the sentient world, and they sense our genuine interest. And as with humans, so with the trees and nature spirits.

The charm is fascination. To be fascinating, be fascinated.

Working with the ideas that follow will help you become a charmer of dryads, so, if your journal is to hand ...

• • • • • • • •

Becoming Familiar with Charming

Write the heading: *Charming*. Under it, list all the things in your life that you would currently call charming. None yet? Imagine what might be charming in a more gracious, perfect life!

How does using the word "charming" make you feel? Decide now to associate it with lightness, gracefulness, pleasure.

Over the next few days, practice noticing or finding things in yourself, neighbours, family, and the world that you could call charming.

Start using the word in your internal monologue. Prime yourself to think "That's charming!" regularly. How many circumstances in your present life does it apply to? Your favourite clothes, plants, social arrangements?

Some things may seem too gross or mundane to be charming—the garbage, for example. But you may find an efficient elegance to the way it is collected regularly and disposed of thoughtfully. While it's not quite charming, it is a necessary part of a charming life.

Devise a charming occasion for yourself within the next twenty-four hours. Charming occasions are special. For example: we drink many beverages, but the special porcelain cup, the exquisite biscuit, sitting in our favourite chair, and viewing a perfect landscape to drink the first cup of the day is a charming ritual. It is a time set apart from worldly cares. A time with space for thoughts, for an expansion of the spirit. Dream up some such occasion to suit your taste. Now do it for a week.

We will cultivate charming
moments in our everyday lives
to acclimatise ourselves.

Next, we need role models who share a living relationship with nature: and they live in fairy tales, just waiting to be noticed. The youthful hero/ines of these stories seem to communicate easily with nonhuman entities: they talk to birds and are protected by trees, horses, and rivers. They are young, telling us that we must cultivate a youthful spirit. They are generous, open-hearted folk who delight in the world, who trust in the best in spite of their poor circumstances, so we will cultivate those attitudes. We call them Jack the Giant Killer, Snow White, Aladdin, Cinderella, and Hansel and Gretel. Their stories tell us that they are charmers.

Their examples will lead us into the woods and to our dryad's tree so lightly that our feet will not disturb the leaf-strewn path and our clothes will not be snagged by thorn and bramble.

We will come into rapport with the
living world, for the ability to charm,
to connect, is deep within us all.

To Sum Up So Far:

    ❁ We will cultivate generosity and acceptance
        to attune ourselves to nature.

Being judgmental is very human and always diminishes us; it is never attractive or charming to any species. We will learn from the trees, the wind, the animals, who all accept that their life just is. Through being with them, we will learn to integrate gracefully all aspects of our lives.

    ❁ We will cultivate lightness of spirit and a sense of joy
        of being in nature.

Being heavy or self-important is not the way to charm or attract. We will develop an attitude as light as the response of leaves to every breeze, which brings an awakening sense of joy.

    ❁ We will evoke from within ourselves those qualities
        that will charm our dryad.

To evoke means to generate a feeling or emotion from within and draw it up into your consciousness. Up until now, most of our evocations—of anger, perhaps—have arisen spontaneously of their own volition. It is a simple process to evoke positive emotional responses consciously, yet it is of huge importance. We will practice throughout every chapter of the book.

Our first connection is through being deeply intuitive—when we allow ourselves time to be. But, because of the species difference, our challenge is how to start the dialogue and make relationship.

Q: How do we start?

A: We look from the dryads' viewpoint.
What would they find attractive?

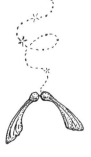

New bonds are formed when two parties have something in common. Fortunately, traditional stories reveal some aspects of the nature of dryads. These tell us what our deep selves already know: that dryads are creatures of strength, integrity, grace, and inner beauty. They flee from aggression; they dance and are associated with music; they are long-lived.

In those old tales, dryads are usually women. Today, though, why would we need to apply a gender to a wood spirit? As we understand gender as a whole spectrum rather than two opposing poles, there is a great freedom in allowing our dryad to be what they need to; they will inform us, but, even then, we do not need to pigeonhole them.

We might think that dryads will feel drawn to and comfortable with people who share some of these characteristics, but that may be rather simplistic. Many humans with more energy than grace and more spontaneity than consideration may crave a dryad companion, and many dryads may be attracted by fiery human energy! There is enough diversity in the dryad kingdom to ensure that we can all be called by a dryad who is attracted either to our similarities or our complementary qualities. We bring our own strengths to share, and, as with inter-human friendships, some seem completely unlikely but just work! Even the most tempestuous person can charm a dryad, and learning more about ourselves along the way is a bonus, making the work fascinating and rewarding.

We must make time for a two-way attraction. Instinctively, we feel a dryad connection will be good for us; it will be a privilege. I'd like to suggest now that it will also be good for the dryad. I believe that all species benefit from positive energetic interaction. How may become apparent later, but all this takes time.

Our sensing selves know that, in charming a dryad, time taken equals joy, so this work should be a keenly anticipated delight. But our rational minds insist that time equals effort, so we need to cajole our bossy brains. To get them on our side, they deserve to understand, logically, why this work is so worthwhile. So here's the science bit:

Scientific research supplies irrefutable evidence of the positive effect of a forest contact, and some findings seem almost impossibly enchanting and magical.

* It is proven that trees "talk" to each other—

* They communicate their needs and send nutrients through an underground internet of fungi: the true world wide/wood wide web.

* Like us, they cooperate and share.

* They warn each other of impending danger.

* Most amazingly, parent trees have a special relationship that enables them to favour and nurture their own young.

* Messages run through the fungal network from the outskirts through to the interior of the deep forest and out again.

* Trees receive carbon from each other, benefitting and donating according to species and season.

* When threatened, trees take action—producing chemical defences against termite infestations, for example, and warning of impending fires.

* Some trees huddle sociably; others maximise access to the sun by keeping their distance so their canopies are all separate.

The forest is a network of quiet intelligence, with ancient trees acting as hubs. Quiet intelligence is a quality to cultivate if we're to charm dryads.

Assuming a reasonable level of health and fitness, then to charm a dryad we will need to go to the tree. If you're not able to do that, there are alternative plans and suggestions. A 2001 survey sponsored by the Environmental

Protection Agency makes salutary reading... Americans spend 87 percent of their time inside, plus another 6 percent in an enclosed vehicle,[1] whilst the average Brit spends 22 hours indoors—equating to around 90 percent of their day.[2]

The message is clear: we should get out into nature more, so if mobility or general health is a concern, then using all contacts/family/carers/friends with cars to help get you out regularly can only be good.

Shinrin-yoku—forest bathing, or visiting the forests to imbibe their benefits consciously—is a simple practice with proven benefits:

- Forests destress us.

- The colours green and blue are restful.

- The quietness feeds our finer senses.

- The forest carries a beneficial elixir: a chemical released by trees actually boosts the immune system.

- Our bodies respond with a lowering of all the stress symptoms that our lifestyles have made habitual.

- Making a regular practice of consciously appreciating being in green nature gives equanimity: it lowers aggression levels and the tendency to depression.

The Japanese government has incorporated shinrin-yoku into their health programme, and the Woodland Trust has recommended it to the British National Health Service. A Polish study[3] has found that just gazing for

• • • • • • • • • • • • •

1 Chris Colin, "Communing with the Forest Bathers," *Outside* (August 2018), https://www.outsideonline.com/2333396/group-cleanse (accessed August 2020).
2 "Brits Spend 90% of Their Time Indoors," *Opinium* (5 October 2018), https://www.opinium.co.uk/brits-spend-time-indoors/ (accessed September 2020).
3 Ernest Bielinis, Norimasa Takayama, Sergii Boiko, Aneta Omelan, and Lidia Bielinis, "The Effect of Winter Forest Bathing on Psychological Relaxation of Young Polish Adults," *Urban Forestry & Urban Greening* 29 (January 2018), 276–283, https://doi.org/10.1016/j.ufug.2017.12.006 (accessed September 2020).

fifteen minutes at a winter forest landscape—so even with no lush greenery—still provoked a significant health response: participants reported feeling strengthened emotionally, restored, and vitalised. In every season, then, nature contact is of benefit.

Fortunate readers can get outdoors without problems, but if that's not possible for you, know now that just gazing at and contemplating nature will also bring mental and spiritual health benefits. Throughout the book we will each, in our own way, work and adapt the suggestions to explore a world full of sentience, relationship, and communication. Whether through a window or in the wild, the natural world and the trees in particular are just waiting for us to join in and take our place as we cultivate our dryad. So, as with anticipating any new friendship, think of the qualities that we will admire in our new friend. Remind yourself of all that the trees give us and what we should be grateful for. Get the journal out and, just looking round your own home, add to the gratitude list …

• • • • • • • • •

19

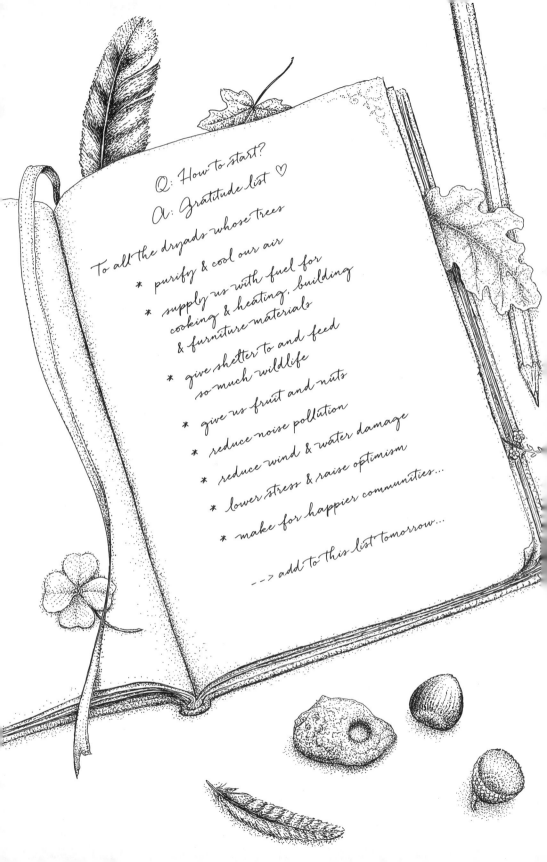

Q: How to start?
A: Gratitude list ♡

To all the dryads whose trees

* purify & cool our air
* supply us with fuel for cooking & heating, building & furniture materials
* give shelter to and feed so much wildlife
* give us fruit and nuts
* reduce noise pollution
* reduce wind & water damage
* lower stress & raise optimism
* make for happier communities...

--> add to this list tomorrow...

TREES AND THEIR dryads, in tune and harmonious with their surroundings, hold a latent power. They are in their right place. They have larger auras, longer life spans, and a different perspective to us. They are of service, donating the raw materials of our lives.

And as well as those physical gifts, they have more subtle gifts for humans. As we prepare to meet a dryad, let us pledge to honour and respect these wise and selfless beings.

Before we go to our first practical exercises, and remembering that time equals joy in this work, spend ten minutes now letting the world slip and dreamily considering what your dryad might be like, and wondering if, somewhere in the green landscape, a dryad is perhaps dreaming of you. Sheltering from the storm under a tree is a good analogy for our life in nature. Let's get close to trees and use the gifts that they are so pleased for us to have.

. . . .

Charm 1 Synopsis

🌿 The first charm, activated by fascination, brings a gift from the forest of intriguing possibilities.

🌿 Activate your yearning. Allow that feeling to flow ahead of you to the trees.

🌿 Relax and trust that when you get to the trees, yearning will start a flow of communication.

Route Map for Charm 1

I allow time; I evoke from my depths;
I cultivate charm and fascination
in all areas of my life;
I breathe in good health from the trees;
I imagine my dryad.

Applying Charm 1

Going to the Trees

*I long to join the
fellowship of the trees.*

IDEALLY WE WOULD now spend a few days walking outside as often as possible. Now, by following the guidelines below, we acclimatise ourselves to looking in a different way at our immediate environment. Acclimatizing also refers to the weather and time; to be serious, we need to experience sun, rain, wind, hail, heat, and cold at any reasonable hour of the day.

If we don't stray too far, it will be easy to keep going until it becomes a habit and a joy. We will be looking with relaxed eyes at every aspect of the natural world, just accepting all that it is and noticing it. If this is in the city, you might wander along a tree-lined road or stroll past lush gardens or discover a local park. Allow yourself just to stroll with no agenda but the aim of seeing, gently and dispassionately, the effect that the simple exercises have on you.

When you are ill, under the weather, or housebound, your habits will change. No one has a good quality of experience when they push themselves past their limits.

If health, mobility, or safety constraints are your reality, then only you will be able to find a sensible, achievable way to connect to the outside world. We all have shortcomings, and some of the most insidious we might not even realise—such as our sabotaging, unhelpful traits and habits. Whether our challenges are physical, mental, or emotional, we will use awareness, attention, and creativity to overcome them. Our unique signature way of engaging with life means that our only option is to craft a personal spiritual path. If you are housebound, an open window can be your outlet to the world of nature. Gaze out every morning to hear, see, and smell the outside world. If you live in a city, in a skyscraper, reach out in your imagination to the nearest huge tree and turn your eyes up to the sun, the sky, and the clouds many times each day. The world will always be out there waiting for your attention.

As with an actual walking experience, the visual/auditory "stroll" that you can travel in your imagination has the same guidelines. We must be relaxed, nonjudgmental, and fascinated to notice all that we can, easily and gently. For a focused walk into fantasy, it is good to lead yourself through a "story" of a forest walk, and to prompt a good experience, we need to tell our story in the present tense; we are telling ourselves that we are actually experiencing it now. Therefore, we don't narrate "There is a wood with the wind blowing through the trees..." but live along with "I am walking through crunching dead leaves in a deep wood; I hear the rustling leaves, and the wind on my neck makes me shiver..." You'll notice that example two is starting to make use of the senses to conjure an atmosphere, of which much more later! When this results in the evocation of an alternate reality in our imaginal realms, we may call this "dreaming green."

Every day, immerse yourself in green nature in your mind; decide now when it would be convenient to do this, and jot it in your journal to remind yourself. It can be helpful to link your practice to your habits—sit down for five minutes to reverie after cleaning your teeth, after showering, as the meal is cooking. By knowing your own temperament, you know what will give you the best chance of success, so you decide. You might use this time to bring to mind idyllic walks, wonderful nature programmes, or happy outdoor scenes from childhood; all these make a valuable visual resource within you. And if these are not your memories, then you have a clean sheet on which to make some from the very next time you go out.

Arrange for the lighting and surroundings to make this easy for you. A special space or chair is not essential but will help; eventually your mood will start to change as soon as you settle down there.

Before You Start Indoor or Outdoor Work

○ Set an expectation that this will be fun and satisfying!

○ Clear a set amount of time—a short time at first so it's easy to succeed.

○ Take some deep breaths.

○ Consciously imagine you are connecting to nature.

○ Allow a tree awareness to arise within you; this is evocation, and vital.

○ Maintain an enquiring, fascinated attitude: *What will you learn?*

○ You've committed your time, so be respectful; take the work seriously but lightly, with pleasure.

Suggestions for Indoor Work

🍁 Find one or two YouTube clips and natural history programmes that you can return to again and again, as if you are taking a walk outside round the same route each day.

🍁 Ditto for background natural music—rain, water trickling, wind, birdsong. Listen to this regularly to promote a feeling of nature within.

🍁 Put a green or golden bulb in a lamp.

🍁 If you have no breathing problems or allergies, scent the room for a woodland atmosphere. You might vapourise essential oils such as pine or rosemary, use a spray, or scent your wrists.

- ❦ Have a special "nature" piece of clothing (a scarf, pashmina, blanket, or wrap) in woodland colours.

- ❦ With the help of friends and family, collect small twigs from your favourite trees and have them present during your visualizations.

- ❦ Ask kids or relatives to bring you things from their walks for your nature table.

- ❦ Start a scrapbook of tree images, the larger the better; find out about them.

- ❦ Consider pictures or a mural of trees for your wall.

THE TIME HAS come; the world—and your dryad—is waiting! As you put on your boots, anticipate the excitement of relating to nature on her terms, not yours. Walk as an enquiring student. Following the guidelines will allow your mind to slow and thoughts to settle. Aspects of nature all work at different speeds, from the life of the mayfly to that of the glacier. Trees, with their longer life span, have a slower time frame to we humans, and they won't speed up for us—and so we settle down ...

Then begin to look around in an enquiring fashion, and there will be a portal: you will find one when you look, and it can take many forms.

Portals and doorways are exciting spaces; even as we walk from room to room, we experience many infinitesimal changes in temperature, humidity, dimensions, and ambience, formed by our associations. Settling into our imaginal world, we can conjure them on the screen behind our eyes. Through our intention, we create portals that can lead us into mystery, into deeper connection, into enchantment. The portal that we find will allow us to shed our everyday concerns like a cloak and tune in to our finer senses. If you are walking in a park, your portal might be an actual gateway; but just as effective would be two trees or shrubs like twin posts for you to step through or an overhanging branch to duck under; it could even be two stands of tall weeds. Keep your eyes open, and be prepared for a slight detour if necessary.

When you have passed this significant point, imagine your footprints pressing light leaf prints on the ground.

With every step, breathe in gratitude and breathe out a request: "May I see wonders."

Switch off your busy rational mind. In the forest, sight, smell, hearing, taste, and touch make up a matrix of sensation that will suffuse your being if you allow it to claim your attention. Imagine the wood or park or forest filling your brain with its green splendour.

Be borne along by the sensations of air and sun and wind. You wish to "dream green" as an extra layer of awareness whilst being fully present and awake and responsive to the physical world. Set your direction by the hints from wild nature to your senses, and be prepared to follow the call of a bird, chatter of a squirrel, a sudden gust of wind, or your attention drawn by a cloud formation. By doing this, you are beginning to choreograph a woodland moving meditation, rhythmic and subtle. Practice this regularly until you feel your inner senses becoming fine-tuned to your chosen walk.

• EXERCISE •

A Seven-Step Process to Your First Tree Communication

When you feel that you are becoming more accustomed to your terrain, you are ready to approach trees conversationally, in a friendly, light way, to develop a joyous relationship. Remember they extend as far underground as above, so notice the ground as well, and use these guidelines to aid your first tree communication.

- ✻ Sense the aura of the trees as you approach; does it change as you get nearer? You might not sense anything, in which case imagine what it would feel like if you could. Enjoy doing that for now and gently encourage yourself. Every try today makes success tomorrow more likely.

- ✻ Pat or stroke each tree in passing if you feel it's appropriate.

- ✻ Notice each tree's particular characteristics. Go closer to examine each one.

- ✻ Whisper your admiration for each particular thing you notice.

- ✻ Let your eyes glance up over the tree canopy lightly, not intrusively.

- ✻ Gaze out from the trunk to see how far the roots extend if they break the soil.

- ✻ Be open to any impressions.

MAKE IT A habit to go through all these stages without expectations, keeping foremost in your mind your enjoyment in the company of the trees for what it is, just as you would enjoy the company of a friend.

Dedicate a couple of pages in your charmer's journal to reminders of the points above, and add to them as you read the later chapters.

Each time you go out, reaffirm your motivation to develop a mutually beneficial friendship with the sentient life of the trees, with a tree spirit: a dryad.

Dryads may appear shy to us noisy humans, but they are big life-forces and representatives of the great spirit of copse, wood, and forest. Every spirit of park or woodland has been developing over several of our human lifetimes, and throughout that time every tree has been an exemplar of witnessing and service to humanity. We do not often consider this longer timescale; enjoy it. It is the beginning of the slow thinking that will attune us to our trees.

We go as students, with much to learn.

These first walks are a lesson in diversity: so very many weeds, flowers, shrubs, grasses, and trees in such a small space! Take your journal and note down how many you can count in a small square of earth: and all coexisting. Check out their species at home if you need to. If you live near an area with poisonous or irritative plants such as poison ivy or nettles, make sure you can recognise them before this exercise. As you become more intimate with nature, feel your understanding of relationships in the world expanding.

After a time, do you sense an attraction for certain trees or feel an aversion or a standoffish attitude from others? Which sized tree feels most friendly and "right" to you? Which species? By their nature, great trees can exude enough energy to make us feel quite nervous: it is a natural response to them and probably an indication to contact a tree of less ancientry at first.

Respect your instinctive feelings and do not harass tree spirits that prefer their own company; unlike humans, they can't move away. Don't wait for a slap with a wet branch or a tripping root to teach you respect. Some species of tree traditionally want less to do with humankind. You may look these up, but, as with humans, the "personality" of a tree is individuated, so it is best to develop a sense for each dryad's response. Intuition is very valuable when human speech is not possible. Your messages will really come from the feeling you get from a tree. Learn to rely on your instincts, but—very importantly—in conjunction with common sense. If you're not confident, keep a respectful attitude and distance whilst you're developing your intuitive muscles.

Being open and allowing for new experiences using intuition and mutual respect will introduce us to the world of fun, enjoyment, and enrichment through nature that will lead to new interspecies friendships.

There will be days when it will be difficult to summon the mental energy for this work. As you either settle into your meditative space or find shoes, coat, and keys, think about why that is. Consider the demands of modern life and how they sap your energy and willpower. Understand that by sticking to this work, you are striking a blow for your soul, your spirit! Remind yourself that the world's demands might become a straitjacket unless balanced by the freedom of nature contacts. That has got to be worth an initial push to get you out. Remember your longings and the urge to connect. Remember your sense of fascinated enquiry. Feel a surge of energy as you do.

Instinctive wandering for a few days, using all the guidelines, in the landscape or the imaginal realms, is the first step to contacting a dryad. It is a relationship that may confirm what your soul already knows—that we are just an expression of nature, and that the whole of the natural world is longing to support us as we expand into all that we can be.

To gain that support,
all we have to do is to ask.

Q: Why search for tree contact?
A: Because we long to move beyond four walls and become intimate with nature spirits.

Charm 2

THE CHARM OF

ACCLIMATISING

33

$\mathcal{W}$e are time travellers.
    Immediately take three
deep, slow breaths as you continue
reading ... if you have happy childhood
memories, think of a scene in nature
from your early life. If that's difficult
for you, let that idea go. Instead, choose
to sense deeply from these suggestions:
    Dappled shadows in summer ...
dramatic evening tree silhouettes ... a

bright November bonfire ... the scent of the forest ... tender leaves you can stroke with childish hands ... the crispness of dead leaves as you kick through them in the autumn.

Feel your spirits lifting as you imagine the scene through sight, smell, taste, touch, and hearing. Spend some effortless time with it, establishing a strong positive reaction, so the feeling floods through your body and mind. It expands an inner imaginal space that you dedicate to your nature connection. To rest with these images for a few moments is intoxicating.

Bookmark this page as an intention that you will repeat it often ...

WRITE DOWN WHAT you reminisced about or imagined in your journal before the feeling is lost. Remembering our early influences or re-imagining experiences we wish we had had in nature is the beginning of acclimatizing. The urban, the disadvantaged, are not locked out by nature, which is always there, a part of us, just waiting for us to make the first move, which is as simple as acknowledging it.

There is a time-honoured way to enchantment through the imagination. As children, our stories included talking trees and dryads. Those early influences of folk, fairy tale, and legend can be potent forces when, as adults, we are drawn to the sense of mystery yet kinship we feel with trees, woods, and forests. As youngsters we are sublimely open to impressions. If we were lucky, we breathed in the narrative strain of the land as we climbed trees and ran down hills. Without conscious thought, we were acclimatizing, becoming in tune. And then we grew, and the pressure of the world's expectations turned our attention to developing into human-socialised and urban beings. While that was necessary, it seemed like an either/or deal. So no longer could we sing with the wind; we became too old for bedtime stories of enchanted bears and talking horses, and Santa quietly faded from our minds. As adults we know that we needn't sacrifice joy and wonder in order to be responsible; we can have it all. We're aiming to return to that state of fresh new appreciation—of our bodies, our lives, and of our lands, our world as an interactive playground, support, and true home—through contact with our dryad. How precious we all are, and how precious is our world! How we long to feel truly acclimatised on this jewel of a blue-green planet. Admiring and loving every local aspect of the world is a good way to start.

Fellow feeling between us and our dryad, once internalised, can act as a portal into other realms. The feeling is the doorway. The more time and space we allow that feeling, the easier we will find it to walk through the doorway into a more profound place. Simply taking regular walks in nature in our locality can take on significance every time, even if we're on the most mundane mission. We are doing our bodies good with exercise and also becoming aware of the possibility of connecting to other realms. We need to be enchanted; it is our focus. We are becoming wonder hunters, questers. We will take every opportunity to further that aim.

To charm, to attract our dryad, we balance the practical and the mystical in our nature to mirror the dryad's own. We acclimatise to the energy of the tree spirits; we learn to sense life again. We had that ability when we were children, and it was reinforced every time we rolled and played with our dog, imitated the cat's stretching, or cried with the clouds when the wicked witch cast a spell on the forest. It is still there, deep within us.

Hopefully, during that first short imagining, you will have noticed leaves rustling, boughs swaying in the breeze, a scent of the deep forest—a feeling of a welcoming message, of acceptance. Look at your journal and note your dominant sense. Do you over-rely on one?

Realising which of your senses you rely on most naturally tells you how you will most likely notice your dryad communicating with you when you are out in nature. But resolve also to work with the others to increase your resources. Cultivate the habit of noticing with every sense both in the imaginal and the real world.

The rest of this charm includes basic guidelines to use throughout the book.

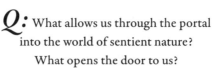

Q: What allows us through the portal
into the world of sentient nature?
What opens the door to us?
A: The spirit of nature itself.

We just have to ask.

Asking doesn't always mean using words: we can ask by the act of evoking the yearning within us: *emotion makes connection*. But we are in the habit of using words to communicate. So now we will form our inner longings by developing forms of words, for bringing ideas into reality via the voice is itself a magical act.

Bring back the feeling of the previous exercise. If it's difficult, do it over again—it only takes a few minutes—and consciously engage with sight, sound, hearing, taste, and sensing. Next time you'll do it with sufficient longing to be in the exercise for every image to be sharp—not necessarily to your inner sight, for many of us do not "see pictures," but to your inner feeling.

Generate this feeling, and from
it allow a request to arise. This
you will use every time you go
out into the landscape. It will be
your personal charm to attune
you to dryad-charming mode.

Your phrase should be simple and encapsulate the essence of what you want at this present moment. If your intent changes or refines over time, so you will alter the wording, always with awareness. If you need extra help, it is there waiting within each of us: as time travellers, we can hark back to when we were open and fresh to the world when we were growing. Going back to that youthful feeling may help you formulate a phrase. We've considered one childhood image, but you may have dozens just waiting to enthuse you. Think back through all four seasons to draw out these memories. Or, if you were deprived of them then, don't you deserve the pleasure of imagining now? If it feels right, look back at your child self with a tender sense of love and a beautiful natural scene in which they can revel. Bring a wonderful feeling of connection back from that brief imagining, which you can use to formulate a request or petition for when you next go out.

Dryad work to do: magical words ♡

Words for my phrase: magic, mystery, enchantment, wonder, verdant, green, spirit, ancient, connection, crepuscular, translucent, liminal.

Note: Keep it simple!
This is not a "mind" exercise!

* May I feel safe and may I see wonders.

* Nature is filled with spirit and so am I. I greet it today.

* Trees fascinate me. For the good of all, I long to connect to a dryad.

→ make 2 more before tomorrow?

Don't force it— see how it goes. Set phone for after supper to think some more about this.

To access the emotions of anticipation and excitement, words must be evocative and excite your imagination. Feel them as you speak them. Play; have fun with all the possibilities you might use.

. . . .

•VISUALISATION•

Exploring Your Inner Forest

Breathe gently and steadily and allow an image to arise so you begin to feel as if you are in the heart of the forest. Look in wonder at its verdant beauty. This is your own imaginal space and you need feel no fear in the forest, although you sense its ancient power. It inspires a great wonder and openness within you. You yearn to be truly at home there—to feel a part of the landscape.

If it feels right, you are here to ask for entry into its mystery. If this is not the time, just relax into beauty for five minutes and return restored.

But if it feels like the right time, then how will you make your request? Who will you ask? Are you in the centre of a grove, a collective of trees that hold the green energy of growth?

Look around to identify a tree that might represent the spirit of the forest for you.

Don't be concerned with words for now; just allow a yearning feeling to arise from you and flow toward the trees. Imagine it leaving you with each outbreath—your own breeze, if you wish, your request stroking the trees. Ask for acceptance, and promise your love and commitment in return.

Then relax and enjoy lazily observing. Trust that your request has landed, that you have been noticed, and that in due course an answer will come and the words you need to ask your landscape and your dryad will emerge. What is the hurry? In the forest there is no hurry. Maybe that is your first lesson.

Breathe with the green, living atmosphere and feel as if the beginning of a communication is stirring. Allow that feeling, a small seed, to take root in the fertile soil of your being. Smile and feel gratitude, then open your eyes.

IN THE DAYS that follow, you might vary your key phrase a little every time you walk to the trees. Play until you find the perfect one and you'll know when you've got it. It will become the key that opens the portal into the natural world for you. Always use it with awareness; it won't work if there's no meaning behind it. We seem born with the habit of becoming stale very quickly, so you may notice that what works today may not be right for tomorrow. We must keep checking our reactions.

Does your phrase requesting an entry into the world of the tree spirits still make you feel calm yet excited? Does it ready you to recognise the miraculous in everyday nature and meet your dryad?

If not, you've reverted back to sleepwalking and need to reactivate your fascination.

Each of us has a wise self that has always known the world is bigger than simply what we see. A great invisible reality informs our physical world. As we start talking to the universe through the trees, we are acting as if all these unseen workings will respond to us, and it's surprising how often that seems to be true! Don't worry any more about this idea for the moment—the trees don't. They are happy and acclimatised to being a significant part of a sentient world, as we soon will be. The important thing is to keep everything we do fresh and relevant to the situation now.

It's in our nature to have expectations, but becoming too rigid or wedded to a specific outcome is limiting. Maybe wants are not right in the greater scheme of things, or, more excitingly, the natural world wants to share wonders that we can't yet imagine. So we don't limit ourselves but cultivate a sense of anticipation. Something wonderful will answer to our requests, even if we don't recognise it immediately. In fact, "May I recognise wonders" might be a useful phrase for you until you get acclimatised to the hints flowing to us.

We are acclimatised to a "bigger, better, brighter" mentality, which blinds us to small, exquisite detail. That way we miss the best things in life, for wonders often come in tiny packages. Our days are filled with a thousand tiny wonderful things that we take for granted when we should be appreciating them. To charm, we will retrain ourselves to notice them. When we fixate on wanting the great mystical experience, we ignore the revelation of the rainbow, the baptism of the dripping trees, the song of the bird at dawn. Just because we notice that birdsong in passing as we turn over in bed doesn't make it less of a blessing. It's all in the noticing. All of these and many thousand others waiting to be noticed are spiritual experiences in the real world. In fact, we habitually ignore what is actually happening all around us.

*Observing closely is the first way of
seeing and making the world, and
our experience of it, enchanting.*

Fixating on wanting an oak connection might mean you miss an invitation from a magical hawthorn, so stay available to the unexpected.

Now you are primed to be a wonder hunter: a charmer who will inspire a dryad into revealing themselves. You are open, relaxed, and accepting. So, let's prepare. If your health precludes you getting out into nature whenever you want to, it is easy to adapt the ideas that follow, for establishing relationship is the same for us all.

Q: How would you make a human friend?
How would you charm a person?

A: You put yourself in their place—
what qualities and behaviour will attract them?

WHEN YOU WALK to a tree, in reality or in an exercise of the imagination, use the following checklist.

Checklist for Approaching the Trees

○ Keep your distance—no one likes being overwhelmed!

○ Use empathy; cultivate a gentle and enquiring attitude.

○ Go prepared to learn, not bustling along feeling you have a lot to give. (This is difficult as we so want to be useful and helpful, but here we are students. We all avoid a know-it-all.)

○ Be the person a dryad would want to befriend. To us, the trees are intriguing and beguiling. How will you intrigue them in turn? By being the one person in a thousand who is genuinely interested? By listening? By being pleased to see them?

· · · · · · · · ·

We have practiced all through our lives on the human population; now we use our skills in nature. Take your time—the trees have longer lives than us. Remember, do not predict, expect specific outcomes, or judge. Nature takes the long view; we just stay neutral and see what happens. Observe; then, at the earliest opportunity, record every nuance of your experience in your journal. The magic is in the detail, most often overlooked and easily forgotten. Freed from what we want to experience, we will be open to what actually happens.

• EXERCISE •

Mirroring the Qualities of a Dryad

This means discovering and encouraging from within ourselves those qualities we wish to find in our dryad. We begin to think of ourselves as alluring and attractive; as having the sort of energetic signature that will attract our dryad. This is possible for all of us. We have unlimited potential; it is a question of waking up those elements that have been dormant. We've been taught to be embarrassed by them: "Who am I to be brilliant, beautiful, charismatic?" Because this feeling is so deeply ingrained into us, we should do this exercise frequently—perhaps each night before sleeping, for, in our essence, we have the capacity to be truly wonderful.

This understanding of self is private; we won't share it with an outside world that would easily misunderstand. Yet acknowledging our latent possibilities will cause a subtle change in the way we perceive and are perceived, even in the mundane world of mortgages and work commitments. It will come from having an expanded viewpoint, a wider sense of our potential.

Do you think that your dryad will be beautiful, gracious, loving, graceful, energetic, calm, accepting, striving, deeply rooted? Which of these qualities will you find and encourage into wakefulness from your deeper self?

We all have aspects of attraction within us, and we can awaken them through our imagination. So before going to search for our dryad's tree, spend a few moments becoming as we imagine a tree person to be. In your own time, with your journal, settle down and breathe with the forest in your imaginal world. Feel yourself as a hunter of wonders embarking on a great new adventure: take your time and evoke all the wonderful qualities that are inside you to awaken gently. Greet your gracious, kind, and vital self, your accepting self that is constantly in tune with nature, and decide to support each positive aspect of your personality as it emerges.

*Come back energised, as if you've
had a bath of green vitality, and
write a list of the qualities you wish
to encourage in your journal.*

....

....

....

....

....

....

CONSIDER THESE QUESTIONS also, before the next time you go walking: How will you find a tree? How will the tree find you? How will you recognise each other?

This is our preparation, but there are no right or wrong answers to these questions. You decide. Make a personal list to take as an *aide-mémoire*.

In our next charming session, we will introduce ourselves to a tree—or, if you are housebound, prepare to go inward to do the same thing. As a preliminary, always breathe with the earth beneath you and the sky around you and affirm that you are a child of nature.

As soon as you can, go on an easy walk and reach a place, a physical place, where you pause and speak your phrase, your request. Breathe with the earth and sky, and imagine your thoughts being carried out on your breath, and then stroll, observing which trees look particularly attractive or welcoming to you; that's all. Record everything whilst it's fresh in your memory.

Take your common sense with you: be safe! You'll be too tense to use your intuitive faculties outside if you don't feel comfortable and secure. And if those senses have been waiting a long time, you'll need to practice before you're confident. Relax; that's fine. Anticipate success.

Allow it to flow. What's the rush? The trees are not going anywhere.

Charm 2 Synopsis

❦ The second charm
   is generated by our
   commitment.

❦ It brings a gift from the
   forest—an expansion into a
   wider green world.

❦ As we acclimatise and
   cultivate attraction, a feeling
   flows ahead of us, priming a
   response from our dryad. We
   trust that this is happening
   each time we go to the trees.

❦ Use your own request, emanating
   from this sincere feeling: "I long for
   the friendship of trees."

Route Map for Charm 2

I request, I greet, I notice and am noticed;
I listen, I feel, I observe, I share, I thank;
I note and record.

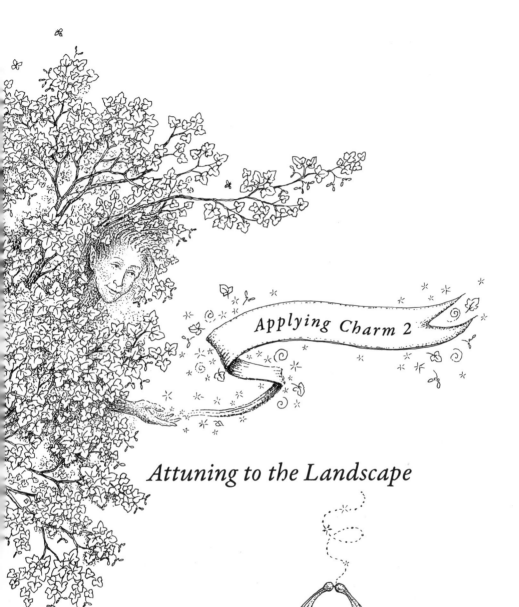

Applying Charm 2

Attuning to the Landscape

*I walk into nature,
both outside and in my
imaginal realm.*

Enchantment notes—

1. Focus on enchantment of trees
2. Use all my senses
3. Use imagination before the walk
   * dim forest light
   * smell of leaves & forest floor   ♡wild garlic!
   * feeling of pure air: "I am a
     wonder hunter! I am at home in
     nature!" (wear green scarf)
                        I respond to nature—
            my dormant senses are awakening!
       → Keep checking this feeling
   throughout the walk. Get it all going
   whilst lacing boots—
                                Yeah!

AFTER THE SHORT intuitive approach of the last charm, where we wandered with fascination, we will now become more focused. Check back to the "before you start" section on page 26 to renew your motivation.

Whether inside or out, nature time is *slowww-errrr*... so slow down... and slow down again... and again. Every time, breathe with the air and the earth and affirm that you are a valid, valued part of nature. By the end of the book, these slow-time exercises may have helped you to reframe your whole idea of your relationship with the world and what you want it to be.

Stop frequently, breathe consciously, and check in with your five senses every few steps to tune into what is actually around you. It is almost certainly a little different to what your mind thinks is there. Maybe you will change your generic idea of "trees: green" to "trees: today, greenish but rusty round each leaf, yellowing underneath." It is not a dramatic change, but it is a significant indication that you are present and noticing what your eyes are reporting.

If you need to be indoors, you're still aiming for an immersive experience. You want your senses to be suffused with the atmosphere as if in the forest. Use the suggestions from the earlier practical work and sink into seeing, smelling, hearing, and feeling with your inner senses, then use the guidelines below. In an inner space you can speed through the exercises, so be sure you allow time for a two-way interaction—time for the response to come. The mind will want to jump in with its interminable inner dialogue, so keep dismissing this gently and focus on a peaceful feeling that will allow images to arise. As we found a physical portal the last time we went onto the land, so slowing and being open to a response is our inner portal to a more profound wisdom than that usually available to us.

> *We are students viewing*
> *with new eyes.*

51

*Every aspect of the world is
precious. The way the myriad life
forms co-exist is miraculous. How
wonderful that we are a part of it!*

Feel your senses sharpening and walk into adventure. It probably won't include a dragon—but maybe two minutes spent watching a snail crossing a path will be just as magical. Every walk can be into an enchanted forest, over a verdant lawn, into whispering shrubs. Every breath of wind might reveal something to your youthful gaze. You may lose minutes contemplating a spider's web or the way nuts or berries hang from a tree.

Whenever you walk or meditate, to give yourself the very best chance of experiencing, make the request you've decided upon out loud. For example, "May I have a joyous experience, and may I see wonders." You'll have realised by now that, if we regard this book as a love song to the trees, your phrase supplies the chorus!

Then, when you walk out and spot a likely tree, one that attracts you, stop! Think! Ask first, as you would of a person. Never omit this. Practicing politeness and respect will be our attitude to the whole sentient natural world. Think of human interactions; we don't stroke a stranger, even if they've smiled at us! Our first encounters with the trees and their dryads are the equivalent of introducing ourselves to other humans and finding out enough about each other to know that we both want to pursue the relationship.

Relax and take your time. Your tree has been waiting for your contact; no need to rush in now. Remember the persona that will be attractive to any potential dryad friend. Breathe with the earth, with the sky, with your dryad, to slow and prepare you.

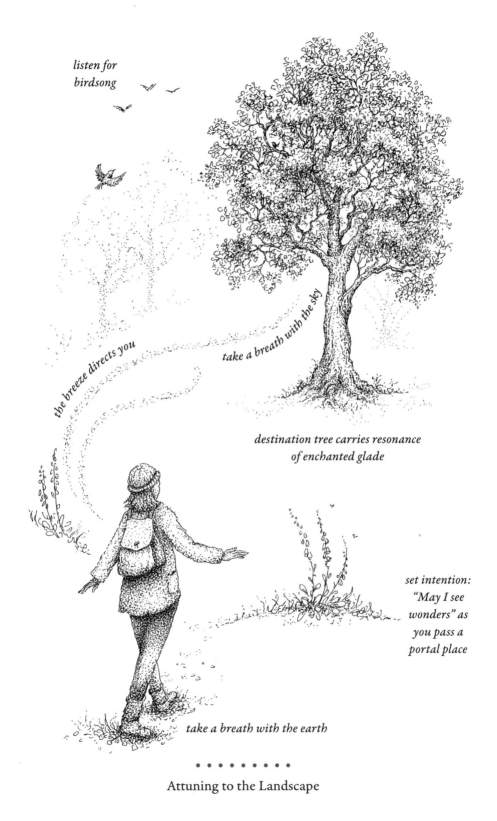

listen for
birdsong

the breeze directs you

take a breath with the sky

destination tree carries resonance
of enchanted glade

set intention:
"May I see
wonders" as
you pass a
portal place

take a breath with the earth

Attuning to the Landscape

Checklist for Connecting to the Natural World

○   Awaken your finer expansive senses from their dormancy
by imagining that that is happening.

○   Do not only stare directly at the object of your attention:
use your peripheral vision; relax to pick up whispers and
glimpses.

○   Pause frequently. Be amazed at how fast you usually walk
(even how fast-paced your meditations might be)!

○   If your intuition suggests a different approach, then try
it. No point listening for whispers and then ignoring
them! Equally, do not follow anything that is barking
mad, illegal, immoral, or dangerous. Your tree might like
to see you nude, but the mums in the kid's playground
will have other ideas. We are social animals, and part
of our respect for sentient nature is respect our fellow
humans and the society that we're a part of, so we obey
its dictums and stay under the everyday world's radar.

· · · · · · · · · ·

We know that making friends, whether human or interspecies, is a mysterious and two-way process: How do we gel with some but not with others? But
always you must listen for a response. And if you don't slow down enough
for your dryad's timescale, your head will be permanently full of questions
and you will never sense a reply, no matter how "loud" your tree is being.
Relax until the rational mind shuts up! Wait for any response that might
come. If your dryad takes their time, well, why shouldn't they? If they don't
respond until you have been visiting for a month, well, you will have proved
something to them of your commitment—and maybe to yourself as well.

Think of ways you can physically relate to a tree that attracts you. You
may not be into tree climbing anymore, but you can certainly lean, stretch
upward, and imagine following the squirrels and little critters scamper-
ing in the upper branches, with boughs bending under your weight before

each leap! Lean on a low-hanging branch and sense the life-pulse of the tree thrumming along it: feel its life force.

If you are inside watching a nature programme or gazing at a mural or poster or out the window at a tree, still try out and adapt these ideas and all the suggestions that follow. You might want to have your diary nearby so you can draw an impression of the tree or the images that arise in response to it. Keep pausing, relaxing, and passing through into a realm where the forest inside you lives: a place of regeneration and nurture. Be as creative as you need or wish to be in your adaptations.

Checklist for Attracting and Being Attracted By Your Dryad

Go to the wood/park/green avenue with feelings open ...

- ○ Follow all the "connection" advice above.

- ○ Evoke a longing for a dryad connection from deep within your green self.

- ○ Feel that the connection has already happened on one level and take your time.

- ○ Keep open for guiding hints that catch your attention from the wind, birdsong, or any natural movement.

- ○ Remember the response might come as a feeling, a sound, a smell, a movement, or a view that suddenly strikes you as particularly vibrant.

- ○ Become aware that you are drawn to one particular tree. If it doesn't happen this time, no matter, no rush.

- ○ Ask a tree if you might approach; sense the response.

- ○ If it doesn't feel right to do this, never mind. Nod hello as you pass, and try again sometime.

○ When you feel a response has come from your tree, you can walk gently nearer and start to discover its amazingness.

If your tree is emanating a strong, friendly feeling...

○ Approach quietly, breathing in connection and breathing out goodwill.

○ Note every nuance of change—temperature, feeling, and movement—as you come within its aura.

○ Introduce yourself to its dryad simply and briefly.

○ Ask to be its friend—to be inducted into the green life of the trees through it.

○ Offer in return your goodwill, time, and attention.

○ Wait for any response—a feeling, a movement of the leaves, a sound—that may come from the outside world but feels significant.

· · · · · · · · · ·

Magic emerges from the detail. To make the point, let's apply a general "trees have green leaves" mentality to making friendships with humans. We don't make a good impression on new people by dismissing them as just man/woman/blond/tall/gender preference; it's diminishing and offhand and definitely not charming. We all want to be liked for our individuality, our particular selves, and so does the dryad and their tree.

To connect, notice more closely and record every specific characteristic of a tree.

Checklist for Our Close Attention

Taking the leaves again—and they are so diverse, even on the same branch!—

- ○ Which are darker/smaller?

- ○ Which are later to emerge than those nearby of the same species, and why? Work it out!

- ○ Where is the tree in relation to the rising sun?

- ○ Notice the bark, the tree's way of growing, its shape, any evidence of human management (cutting, coppicing, pollarding[4] and so on). Look, look, look and notice, notice, notice. Trees are fascinating!

- ○ Study the bark, the leaves/flower/fruit, shape...

- ○ How far do the roots extend? What is the spread of the canopy? How far down do the boughs droop?

- ○ Which bits of your tree can you touch? What do they feel like?

- ○ Which bits touch you as you walk underneath it?

· · · · · · · · · ·

How many notes and sketches will you have in your journal by the time you go home tired and happy?

· · · · · · · · · · · ·

4 Coppicing and pollarding both cut trees back, often to encourage new growth. Coppicing happens at ground level whilst pollarding is cutting back the head of the tree.

My tree's special characteristics:

Tree type: Birch

Location: Edge of local park

Single/group? Set apart from stand of limes &
copse of birch in the extreme corner

Appearance: Very well grown; beautiful
symmetrical shape; very graceful compared
to copse

Bark: Silver-white but with regular furrows,
looks a bit like tall asparagus stems

Leaf: Just coming; small bright green, tender,
spear-shaped.

Notable: Black lace twigs and drooping branches
still very prominent; will be covered within a
month?

Approx. spread & height: Around 30-40 ft?
*go back & check

Now write the story: "How I connected to
the birch"

Bringing It All Back Home

If it's a fine day and fine terrain, you can continue work under your tree or it might be back at home; you choose. If you are at home, you should have your diary, pencils, and pens by you. We've reached the stage of checking and recording. You might find the internet very useful in identification and to see your tree at all seasons. Note what you actually saw, felt, heard, and the sense of your encounter. How creative can you be? Will you use photographs, bark rubbings, leaf pressings, or sketching and potato prints, or all of these?

. . . .

Our sample journal entry might help you with some headings—or devise your own. You are still exploring, so no need to limit yourself to one tree, especially if you are working from home.

You'll have noticed that all of this is about the tree, not the dryad. As with other friendships, we start with people's physicality and then get to know them through personality, temperament, and the subtler senses. We are honing our super-senses, for through the physical, we come to the spirit that is an essential part of the life of the tree. Sensitizing ourselves is essential to the process of dryad charming.

A last thought for this charm's practical work: I've suggested that you should look with peripheral vision, at the very edges of your sight, to try to perceive energies that are other than entirely corporeal. When you do this, if you imagine or sense that you may have seen something on the very edge of your vision, something without a clear outline and just a suspicion of a shape, colour, movement—have you ever wondered how *we* appear to the energetic beings of nature? Maybe we're just as spectral and elusive to them as they to us at the moment. Hopefully, as we walk with awareness, we will become more visible to them, more real, as we wish them to become to us.

To charm, we acclimatise and attune
ourselves to the ambience of the forest.
May the trees make us welcome!

Q: Why is appreciating and having fun part of dryad magic?

A: Because it is vital to experiencing life in abundance.

Charm 3

THE CHARM OF TRUE APPRECIATION

*B*reathe deeply. Now, in your imagination, walk through a park and become aware of a breeze that holds the strains of an elusive song from another plane.

The music is tantalising; feel that you are hearing it with your inner ears in subtle vibrations.

Your feet grow lighter as you are caught up on the swirling wind,

dancing toward a tree whose branches
are rising and falling in invitation.

You circle around the trunk, leaves
and twigs brushing your hair as you
hold the trunk to move and swing,
clinging one-handed to a tall branch to
twist yourself underneath, gazing up
to the green canopy of leaves turning
above you and dancing, twirling, to a
melody heard in this imaginal realm,
until it dies away.

You slow to a stop, breathing deeply,
and lean against the trunk until your
heartbeat returns to normal.

THIS IS THE fun charm! Lightness is the watchword as we explore our creative expression. Some parts may be out of our comfort zone: that's fine. Be gentle but firm—do challenge yourself at your own pace. Moving into a new understanding requires a constant willingness to progress.

Having found the tree inhabited by your dryad, bear in mind that you alone have not made the choice: cultivating that feeling that you have chosen each other is an important part of changing our relationship with the world. Don't worry if you haven't yet connected to a particular tree/dryad. Act "as if" and continue softly encouraging this with the tree that seems the friendliest by frequently visiting with a sensitive approach. Sometimes we have to act in order to bring our imaginal reality into the real world in the right way. Any friendly tree will be glad of your notice and regard, so good luck!

Making the acquaintance of one dryad will be sensitizing you to all its companions. Through the simplest means—just walking and pausing with awareness and openness—you're discovering that every copse is a group of distinct personalities and lives, with differing wants and needs; we will return to this idea later.

Hold all of this at the periphery of your awareness. For now, your job— and joy—is to slowly become the charm in order to build your relationship with your dryad. As with making human friends, you do this by being genuinely and infinitely fascinated by every process of your tree: by questioning and then allowing time for a response.

Be respectful of the tree's longer life. From the dryad's point of view, there is no hurry to cultivate their human. In one of your intuitive "conversations," you might explain our shorter life span to explain the speed and hurry that they will undoubtedly sense. When you are ready to explore relationship with a particular dryad, feel that you are a quester who has arrived at your first destination; now is the time to slow into the next stage.

We do that by visiting often, honouring time passing in our respective spheres. Each time reflect on what events in life, compared to that of your tree, have transpired between visits. Feel that your tree spirit is becoming accustomed to being visited and is beginning to know you. Are there any indications to support that feeling? Look, listen, and sense to become aware of them. Affirm that "I know, and I am known." This is not an arrogant mantra but one that sets out an aspiration as a fact—one way to plug into magic!

We are gradually becoming people who attract the attention of the trees; we are light, joyous, and capable of being in the moment. And, hopefully, we will begin to express that in our everyday lives as well.

Mary Oliver exactly captures the quality of exuberance for life in fullness and abundance:

> When it's over, I want to say: all my life
> I was a bride married to amazement.
> I was the bridegroom, taking the world into my arms.[5]

Read that again, out loud and slowly—how does it make you feel? Hopefully you are smiling softly, maybe nodding; you feel inspired and aspirational; it opens a door to a larger way of living life. How would it feel to be that intimate with life? It reactivates that original yearning that started us on this quest; which, although dormant, still disturbs our equilibrium. We need to love life more deeply. There is a sense of balance and peace when we obey the insistent urging of that whisper. Communicating with the trees keeps this feeling awake, and if we're to fulfil our true creative potential, it is our joy.

. . . .

5 Mary Oliver, "When Death Comes" in *New and Selected Poems* (NYC: Beacon, 1992), 10.

The overwhelming involvement in life the poem describes is interactive, a breathing out of intense love and drawing in of wonder. It is the interest that keeps one still for hours watching wildlife—that forgets itself in the fascination of the moment. If the woods, the park, and your garden inspire this in you, then all the work you will do will strengthen this feeling.

> *There is no way of anticipating*
> *what gifts your dryad might*
> *give you in return for your love,*
> *appreciation, and commitment.*

Like any human good friend, a friendly tree spirit may supply you with just what you need in the moment—support, love, healing, a good talking to that brings you back to a sense of perspective (trees can be stern as well as loving)! We'll look later at the mythic pointers to the gifts of the trees, but for now, we want to go out unencumbered by expectation: to see and sense in a light and easy way the extraordinary aptitudes our dryads might have.

Fun and the creative arts are an intrinsic part of true appreciation, which often bubbles over into the need to create, so let us now consider dance and song. Perhaps they don't have a huge part of your life? If not, let that be rectified now, for "fairies [we insert the word 'dryads' here!] never say 'We feel happy': what they say is, 'We feel dancy.'"[6] Humans have the same reactions. After trauma, we feel frozen, immobile; at joyous times, we move flexibly and gracefully. This is the charm that starts you moving—your hands and arms, your trunk—gracefully, swaying parts of your body to emulate a tree's movements. If you are chair-bound, it can be as gentle as you need it to be. Just try moving, as you visualise a tree, and then notice how you feel. Is it freeing? Do you feel lighter afterward? Just rolling your ankles and wrists can be enough to key you into tree energy if you use your imaginal sight at the same time to see your movements as you wish them to be.

. . . .

6 J. M. Barrie, *Peter Pan in Kensington Gardens* (Bath: Arcturus, 2018), 44.

What music did you like as a child and adolescent? Try humming this (or whatever you now like if your tastes have changed) as you go about your daily routine. But never underestimate the magic of songs heard when we were fresh and young and taking in the world in great big gulps; they can still affect us profoundly. Move more lightly as you hum. The European Waldorf (Steiner) schools use simple chants and songs to connect activities for very young children. Their use introduces a rhythm and harmony that little ones respond well to; maybe we could adopt a similar system? Have you a song you sing along to, to energise you for big household jobs? Why not try it and see the effect?

Traditional sources tell us that dryads have a natural affinity with these arts, and we see that they love to dance in their trees in time to the rhythm of every breath of wind. Accessing things lightly and with joy is important; no heavy worthiness will ever charm a dryad! Including dance and music into our mindset, our toolbox of resources, will gradually reeducate our minds to include all creative arts. At the moment it may be well outside our comfort zone, so start minimally and have fun but hold it as a serious intent. This is one very important way to relate to the natural world: to encourage a two-way conversation without words. Have you hummed, whistled, or sung softly to your dryad yet? If not, that will be your next step when we journey back into the forest.

Have you your diary handy? Druids find thinking in threes helpful to fix things in the mind, so take five minutes to drift into your inner territory. Think of three things that would allow you to develop a keener relationship with your dryad to emerge, and jot them down. As you'll aim to do them every day, they must be simple and short. To become a tree person, we need constantly to check in with the natural world, and we don't do that in a shopping mall.

· · · · · · · · ·

....

....

....

Three Simple Things

* Spend 5 mins a day outside (walk from bus to work, walk round the block at lunch time, go out into garden at night)

* Chat to the world daily, specifically the elements & the weather.

  Just like I talk to my dryad: a focused intention, whispers, out loud, in my mind. Always from a feeling in my heart.

* Start a compost heap to get me out with the garden waste each day!

Note: when too unwell, open the window; adapt ideas but keep the spirit; get out more! Keep changing these (or adding to them). Keep it simple. Set the phone alarm to check in on awakening those dormant feelings!

The guidelines from the earlier charms will help you formulate your list— and remember always to say hello and give compliments. We are building strong ties with the world.

Q: How can I fit all this into my life?
I'm really busy all the time.

A: Little and often, little and often—
the value of this work is to give us a
more relaxed sense of space and time.

Q: Any tips? I'm finding it pretty difficult.

A: You might still be clinging to the idea that to
be of value, things must be difficult. Not so! Use your
existing lifestyle as the structure and gently insert simple
exercises each day. Soon you will eagerly anticipate these
short times as a valuable respite from the cares of the
everyday world, and finding time will become easier.

· · · · · · · · · ·

For now, what do you already do, and which new ideas fit most easily into that template? What do you do that you know is a waste of your time? Drop it! This work will help you become more aware of your own rhythm of life, which is a wonderful thing. Actions can—and should—be as simple as saying good morning/night to the world out the window each time you clean your teeth. We humans really want things to be complex, but many really important things are surprisingly simple.

If you have mobility issues, know that physical proximity to our tree isn't necessary to speak to its dryad: visualise her in her tree in her current state—being rained on, dancing in the wind—before winging a "good night" and "good morning" through the ether every day. Check in on a visit if and

Dancing with a Dryad

when a relative or friend can help you get out. Ask if the messages are getting through, and take the opportunity to ask your dryad about a style and form of daily greeting. And if you can't go, relax and just trust. Everything you do with focus and sincerity in this world has an effect. Every experience is real on its own level and has an effect that benefits both you and the world of nature.

It is indisputable that music and song can lead us to magical realms and support us when we're there. They can plumb the depths of our psyche, which is why they are used to reach coma patients.

We are acclimatizing to the expanded sense of well-being that contact with a dryad brings, so the music we choose will resonate with and support that feeling. Songs specifically about trees and dryads are rarer than hen's teeth, but we all have songs that evoke that feeling of being with the trees— be that dreamy, magical, energised, or as if a portal is opening to another magical space. Our uniquely personal response to music makes it impossible to recommend our choice for anyone else. What is important is our response of relaxation and well-being within; an awareness of a greater life that holds all sentient beings safe. Your music may be energetic, sleepy, mystical; your choices may be instrumental; you might just listen to a recording of nature sounds. Have fun. Play your sounds whilst looking at trees or pictures of trees or trees in your imagination. Perhaps your tree is a rocker or a folkie? With play, joy, and application, we build a store of resources to keep key into that "larger" person we are gradually becoming. In the exercise section, we will experiment with praise phrases as the start of poems or songs. Who knows— we may even dance!

Getting "out of our heads" means noticing the stranglehold the rational mind has as the only interpreter of the world and deliberately choosing to give our intuition a chance. For an harmonious experience of life, we need both in a fluctuating, appropriate balance.

HOW'S IT GOING? Play is to the fore, and practicing holding things—plans, ideas about working with your tree—lightly. Most of us have one plan at any given time, which becomes out-of-perspective important. If we hold several at a time, then we don't become rigid over their importance; we can discard or adapt as necessary. Often, by holding lightly, we can achieve far more. Modern life encourages us to live in a cut-off headspace of plans, worries, and angst, but living with our hearts and bodies, emotions and feelings, as well as our abstract thoughts, magical interaction starts to happen.

None of this work should make you feel stressed, worried, or overloaded. If so, step right back and consider what is happening. You'll probably find that you'll have applied "everyday" thinking to it: that work is serious and stressful and that nothing is achieved without effort. With dryad work, the effort is fun; the exercises are dictated by what is happening in the world around you.

> *Part of the message of this charm*
> *is appreciation of what actually is.*
> *We learn to love and grow from our*
> *trees in all weathers and seasons.*

How do you respond to your dryad when the sun's shining brightly in winter or summer? When it's raining or windy? When evening is approaching? Let us take some time in our imaginal world to find out.

The Dryad in All Weathers

Settle down, becoming comfortable and breathing regularly, until you are ready to sink into an imaginative state. See yourself going on a walk and playfully, lightly, your dryad is making itself known to you...

The scene will shift several times, but you will be ready and happy with each change. Feel your footsteps on the earth as the scene forms around you.

Greet the dryad of your tree: "Hello, it's [your name] and it's lovely to be here again." Sing softly; hum; walk a circle around, touching the trunk; dance and skip in your approach; blow a kiss; gaze up through the branches.

Ask your dryad, "Will you show
me your differing moods?"

Stand at the periphery of your tree's aura and reach out as the sun shines and light pours through the leaves. What atmosphere emanates from your dryad? Can you see their expression in the shining beams? Bask in the atmosphere for a moment, and feel the tree responding to the sun's nourishment.

Notice that the sky is changing... rain is coming. The clouds are travelling fast, and you feel the excitement of the gusts of wind that drive them along. The branches begin to move more vigorously, clashing musically, and the first heavy drops of rain splatter on the leaves.

Does your dryad seem strong and enduring? Do you want to shelter under their canopy? Just ask, and feel the protection they can give. Watch the water runneling down from the joints of the trunk and boughs. Think of the myriad life forms within the bark of the tree. Feel the dryad's joy in the movement that the wind allows. Feel energised by the atmosphere, by the freshness of the air.

The rain clouds move over slowly to reveal a glorious sunset. You are still, listening to the dripping leaves, and the evening is coming. Shadows gather. You are in a mysterious cave of leaves, but you feel completely safe.

Imagine your dryad sitting at the junction of the largest branch and the trunk. Share the space with them for a few minutes, then sense that they are ready to sink into tree dreaming. It is time to go after a whispered goodbye and thank you. Bring back a tree-sense of being always in the right place, whatever the circumstances.

You are completely separating from your dryad, consciously, to write up your experiences now. You can always bring to mind their feeling of tree sleepiness to enjoy, perhaps when you need help sleeping.

. . . .

Providing we act always with integrity, there is no right or wrong in any of the charms. If life is very stressful, then your mundane responsibilities must be your priority. Sort them out as well as you can, leaving this work until you have space for it. Hopefully what you've already done will be helpful in your everyday life.

If you find music you love that attunes you to your dryad, if it transports you, then it's right for you. Make a habit of playing it until the next song fires your imagination. When you visit your dryad in actuality—as suggested in the next section—your choice will be in the moment. You cannot prepare far in advance, for how will you know how bitter or mild the weather? How hot the sun and how strong and noisy the wind? The learning is to go out with no expectations but a preparedness to interact in the moment. By this approach, our visits can act like spiritual caffeine on our psyche; they recharge and energise us.

In charm 3 we are charming
a dryad by cultivating true
appreciation of all we can be.

If we wish, we can extend the suggestions—of using music, of dancing—by remembering things we loved as children but might have neglected in our adult lives, and maybe by remembering things we would have loved if school hadn't put us off them. One student for whom this is true has now taken up painting in her seventh decade and is finding it extraordinarily fulfilling. I can't know what skills you might want to revisit or what joyful dreams are dormant within you, so just run free with the idea that you are a creative being.

Do what makes you joyful and
take that true appreciation out
to the whole inspirited world.

Trees are not demanding. We have no need to be good at any art, dance, song, or movement. We are not performing for another human. We set our intent to commune with our dryad and then allow ourselves to flow into the activity, suspending all critical appraisals, and just enjoy ourselves, practicing the art of true appreciation of fullness of life in that moment.

Charm 3 Synopsis

❦ The third charm is generated by our appreciation and joyful dance and song.

❦ It brings a gift from the forest: the pleasure of being in the immediacy of the moment.

❦ We stretch our capabilities to become the fluid, graceful charmer who will tempt the dryad to dance with us. We provoke surprise and delight from our dryad with our

daring; our dryad, in turn, will be intrigued and wish to know more about us. We both sing and listen to their song.

Route Map for Charm 3

I follow my instinct; I know and am known: remembering past joys, I dance; celebrating the marvels of nature, I sing and am enriched; I thank: I note and record.

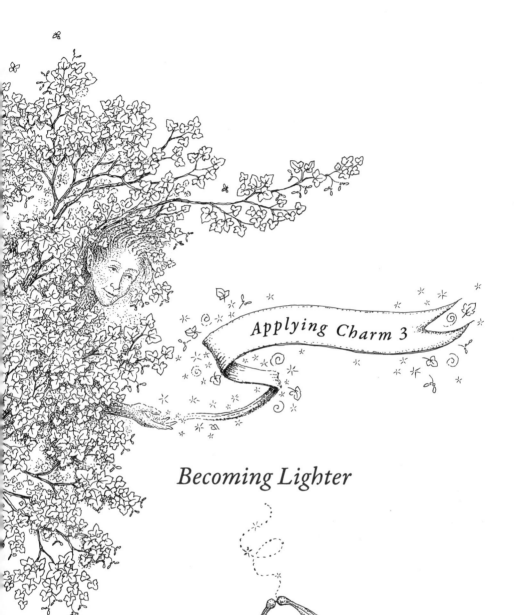

Applying Charm 3

Becoming Lighter

I am light and swayed
by the breeze; I am firm
and rooted in earth.

FOR THIS SESSION, we'll concentrate on appreciation, lightness, and joy. If going out is difficult, it can be difficult to access a joyous feeling, but dryad contact in the imaginal realm can be hugely helpful in developing this attitude, and then it will be easier to evoke it when friends/relatives/carers help you actually visit a special tree. Be gentle with yourself, and allow yourself to relax into a deeper meditative space where your restrictions are not so overwhelming. Lose expectations: with every exercise you will have done a wonderful thing, and you will have primed yourself fully to experience the benefits of nature when you do get out.

Even on the shortest walk, evoke an attitude of lightness and joy, as if you were about to sing or dance. The more we do this in nature, the easier it will be to replicate that feeling whilst doing the housework; we want it to become habitual. Indoors, it's easy to forget. The green life of the tree spirits becomes a part of our makeup through frequent recollection. But you will find hundreds of opportunities to tune in once you set in place little reminders. Take a regular five minutes—after coffee, before supper, as the light fades from the living room window—to focus intently on whatever natural aspect catches your interest (the spider on the ceiling?). That's enough. Often it will trigger memories of other skyscapes, other insects, from your regular walk and take you a little beyond the here and now, just for a few breaths.

The gifts we are giving to our dryad are of time and commitment. A thousand one-minute thoughts are far better than an occasional hour and are much easier to make part of a habit. To get on the dryad's wavelength, on this particular walk we will give especially the gift of creativity and joy—an attitude that awakens our desire for singing and dancing.

Checklist for Remembering the Guidelines

- ○ Keep an awareness of the possibility of communication in the back of your mind.

- ○ Slow down (the golden rule)!

- ○ Breathe, look, listen, feel, and smell the environment.

- ○ Through what you're observing, enter into conscious relationship with the world.

- ○ Introduce yourself every time, even through the kitchen window.

- ○ Name all the aspects of the landscape as you greet them in passing. Name them out loud. A nod can suffice if there are others around, but we all appreciate being called by name.

· · · · · · · · · ·

As with all folks, human or nonhuman, greeting, appreciating, and saying hello is a charming, gracious habit, so do use the expression you crafted earlier. You can change the three things you noted in the last charm to keep yourself interested and fresh, maybe every week.

Always, *always*, observe and experience in equal measure. Stay geared to recognizing a response. This is not an idea conjured up only "in your head" but a dynamic relationship we are forming. Only a bore keeps talking "at" people—human or tree—without wanting an answer, and we all run a mile from them. So be quiet and open to receive impressions respectfully.

To communicate with our friend the dryad, let's now consider also their living environment: a world peopled by water, rock, and weather and affected by the turning of the seasons. So as we open our senses, we may get replies from sources we hadn't even considered—weeds, for example. Or the tiny pebble that still manages to make us stumble. What is it telling us? To deviate from the path? To pick our feet up? That it wants to be moved? People who work with stone—for example, making stone circles—have hundreds of stories of happy

79

stones, reluctant stones, and so on. Sensitising to our dryad is the beginning of a life-long adventure of attuning to the whole world. But for the moment, at the beginning of the journey, we simply need to be open and remember that a walk in nature should always be viewed as a two-way—or a hundred-way—exchange.

> *If you are not listening and sensing*
> *and getting at least as much back*
> *as you are giving out, then you*
> *need to readjust the balance.*

It's worth writing this in your journal and rereading before every walk. We all work too hard and give out too much when we're eager to make progress, but a one-sided conversation very soon runs out of steam. Stop pushing, relax, slow down, and practice listening.

We've danced in imagination—now, if you feel ready, is the time (discreetly) actually to dance with your tree: we can do this! Embarrassed? Not steady on your feet? On a mobility scooter? Then know that a single step or movement, taken with intention, can be a dance. A takeaway coffee or water bottle in hand gives us a reason for slow wandering, observation, and circling the trees that renders us largely invisible in an urban park or wood. Who will notice if we skip occasionally? Who else—if they even notice us, which is unlikely—will realise that the small jump or swerve round an obstacle is, in our imagination, a glorious dancing leap, glide, and chassé to greet our tree with a dance. No one will hear our humming...

If you are housebound, this exercise is easily adaptable, and regardless of ability, this is way out of our comfort zone for some of us. Let's go easily and with enjoyment.

Moving with the Dryads

Getting Ready

Start your conscious breathing and quickly and strongly evoke your "tree-ness." If you are happy to allow it—for you are always in charge—allow an awareness to form of a green current reaching out to your tree even before you see it, whether you are doing this in nature, with a book or photo, or on a screen.

Going to Your Tree

Feel drawn on this green current until you are face to face with your tree in reality. Once there, see (or imagine that you see) the green haze of its energetic body and pause to ask permission before you step into it. Dance and skip in your approach or feel dancy and skippy in your movements. Then pause, say hello, and allow a small thread of melody to arise.

Relaxing Into the Exercise

Sing softly, hum, walk a circle round it, touch the trunk. All the while, be relaxed, observe closely, and feel for a response. Imagine your dryad willing to dance with you in their own reality. The movements of boughs, twigs, and leaves are expressions of the dryad's dance; perhaps they might respond to your movements? Blow a kiss; gaze upward; feel you are in a green tent of leaves; allow a chant or poem to arise—just two sentences will do: or just talk to your dryad, praising its tree; sit at the base of the trunk, lean back, and relax.

If there would be too many observers, do these in imagination, then wave in passing and send a promise to be back very soon.

Praise for my dryad's tree (memorise?)

* Greetings, dear green one!
  Your boughs and leaves make
  a green mysterious tent of leaves,
  keeping me safe in your dim
  shadows

* I praise you, darling birch, for
  your supple form and dancing
  twigs; I honour you with dance.
  Make my movements graceful as
  I circle you...

Play with some rhymes?

* Green leaves, trunk of silver,
  and furrowed bark; I greet the
  dryad stirring now, a spirit and
  a spark.

Use these tomorrow: 1st as greeting, 2nd
before dancing, 3rd during-if I can remember
all. Then sit by the trunk and feel for any
response. Slow down!

Finishing: Walk to the edge of the canopy,
turn, say goodbye and consciously separate &
distance self from the dryad as I walk away...
Don't forget this or the thanks!

Embracing dancing and singing as a part of your life—even if a very private part!—is a matter of perception.

Q: Have you been told that you have two left feet? Do you feel that you're floundering? How on earth do we start to lose our inhibitions, forget our stiff bodies, and dance?

A: Start by harnessing enthusiasm; your dryad will love you for it, so evoke and try the simple ideas below.

· · · · · · · · · ·

Start in bed, or in the chair, or stretching when rising. Use intuitive swaying movements—copy tree movements as if you were a dryad. Let your forearm be a supple branch; your fingers, twigs; your legs and trunk the fluid expressions of a tree moving with the wind. Use every tune on the radio as an excuse to move rhythmically. Combine this with humming your favourite tune and suddenly you will be dancing, in whatever way is comfortable. Making friends with our bodies, whatever their limitations, is a part of this whole process.

Move in this way before every task, at every break; stretch and sway every time you leave the computer. Call your dryad to mind and make a praise phrase—have your journal to hand to note these down as you conjure them. To charm, we need to be truly appreciative: we feel our affection growing for our bodies as an essential part of the natural world.

Play with singing these phrases as you dance:

✻ Like a tree, I am a bridge; I connect the earth and sky;
   Burrowing like badgers deep, reaching like the birds that fly.

✻ From root to tip, I sway with the wind,
   I reach to the sky, I bow to the earth.

✻ Waking with joy, I sing the song of my tree,
   Sap moving, breeze blowing, renewing me.

❦ Dryad of this tree, your speech rustles with every breeze;
May I hear your music; may I sing with you.

❦ Respected ancient oak, your wide trunk is my backrest;
Your roots are my chair; I ask to dream with you awhile.

❦ Hail to the scent of your flowers, magical apple dryad;
Thank you for this springtime blessing.

❦ My dryad peeping through the leaves
With rustling, dancing magic weaves!

❦ I dance for joy, for life, for love;
My dryad joins in high above.

❦ Straight as a tree, wide as its boughs I whirl,
Rooted yet fluid I wheel and spin and swirl!

• • • • • • • • •

Time for a check-in, for our new ventures are often scuppered. It's rarely done maliciously, but our confidence is knocked by the response from the outside world, which usually scoffs at anything not usual. Imagine for a moment an old aunt laughing and saying, "What do you think you look like?" She's a nice person, she means well, but because *she's* thrown off-balance by what you're doing, she wants you to return to your "normal self" as soon as possible, and she's decided what "normal" is. Do you see how insidious that is? That early message strikes at our confidence, and we keep replaying it through our lives—until we become aware of it!

So, before we go any further,
I'll tell you: you look wonderful.
Your authentic, connected self
is waking up and shining.
Well done!

Sketch how you imagine yourself to be, and stick the picture on your fridge to remind you.

When you feel acclimatised, take your creative, light appreciation for another walk to your dryad. Let joyful emotion fuel your actions; decide it will be fun. If you're still self-conscious, stiff, or finding movement a problem, just move your fingers and wrists and stretch gently, setting your intent that it is an amazing, freeing experience. Whatever you are happy and able to do will be enough, so do it with awareness and enjoyment.

Q: But I can only shuffle; how can that be
amazing? It feels not nearly good enough.

A: No matter how simple or shuffly your dance
actually is, your magical imagination is suffusing you
with the feeling of dancing with your dryad.

Q: But just walking is all I can do...

A: So you will make your steps as light and precise
as you can as you approach your dryad, as a dancer
would. Then lean or sit against your tree and visualise
the dance that is happening internally. Gifts are not only
material; give the thought as a gift to your dryad.

· · · · · · · · ·

Forget thinking that you're clumsy: walk as if not only the earth but also the air is supporting your every movement. Indulge your imagination as you approach: you are as graceful as your tree, and they recognise and appreciate that. Reaching the trunk, greet your dryad and invite them to join you...

•EXERCISE•

Sharing Movement

Start slowly, feelingly, so that this is an interactive dance, not you impos-
ing something. Every time you move, pause to check for any response, either
physically, in movement or sound, or in the feeling you are getting. Sense the
twigs that are reaching out to be brushed. Feel when any movement is right,
then:

🍁 Hug the trunk, ducking under any leaves that will
kiss your brow.

🍁 Lean on a low bough and stretch your arms along it;
feel its living energy!

🍁 Reach for a bough that you can use to pivot and
spin around.

🍁 Sense your tree holding the dryad's spirit.

🍁 Hum a tune or take your rhythm from the breeze
that sways the leaves.

🍁 Thank your tree and separate from it fully when it is
time to leave.

• • • • • • • • •

In imagination, you can dance around your tree as wildly, as impossibly, as
you wish, using every part of the tree as a partner. With no limitations, feel
the freedom of leaping impossibly to swing up to the crooks of the trunk and
branches; see energy lines like tightropes helping you, and rest there, high
above the ground.

When you are outside, a dance can be as simple as a stepping walk around the trunk three times, with senses engaged and focused on your partner. Try gazing sometimes at your feet, to see the earth turning beneath you, then to the tree canopy, spinning above, with glints of sky like twinkling dryad eyes through the leaves. Slow; stop, and feel yourself and your dryad as the still centre in a turning universe: a beacon of calm as your muscles relax into a tranquil state and your breath returns to normal.

Thank your dryad and see yourself as completely separate from your tree and wholly yourself. Your body reasserts itself and lets you know that it is time to end. Walk to the far extent of the boughs, turn, and say goodbye, leaving only your thanks and a shared memory.

After both exercises, bring yourself fully down to earth with food/drink as you record the event.

We are inhibited by three things in dancing: appropriateness and social convention, ability and attendant inhibitions, and physical mobility. Acknowledge and honour them all: don't try to be what you're not, but share movement and enjoyment with the tree in your own way.

Lastly, what do we sing? How do we decide? Well, if it's evening, why not start with a lullaby? Most of us remember one, or a nursery rhyme, from childhood. With experimentation we pique our dryad's curiosity: we want to keep nature fascinated and fascinating, so ring the changes. Nature's sounds will give you a lead: if you hear a bird sing, try whistling a response; "woooo" back to the wind down the chimney, and let that sound trigger a simple movement in your body; skip with an errant breeze or spin to take in the whole cloud cover or blue of the sky's dome.

Every instant response is a miniscule
interaction with nature throughout
the day. Each says to a world
waiting to hear from you, "Hello,
how are you? What a beautiful day;
thank you, I love being here!"

Many of us feel the lack of loving contact with other humans. We suffer because we think that human/human connection is our only choice, but the natural world is always there, a loving presence waiting to be acknowledged. So communicate constantly, privately, and with discretion: things do not have to be overt to be very real experiences. Never pass near your tree without sending love and blessings. Always trust the message is getting through and relaxedly listen for any response.

You can use any simple form of more observed breathing with all these exercises; it's up to you to craft what you do. Such techniques can ground, steady, and make it easier for you to switch emphasis from the everyday to a more numinous world. Dancing naturally makes us notice our breathing—part of a growing body awareness. It beds us into being present in the moment rather than "floating" in a rational-mind awareness that is like sleepwalking through life.

To charm, to dance and sing,
we need lightness of spirit:
may our dryads love the joy
of our creative expression!

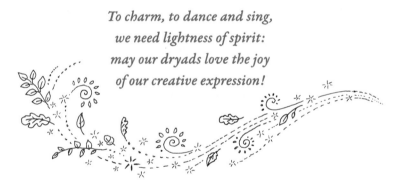

Q: Why do we look to heritage and lineage?

A: Because we long to belong, to feel rooted.

Charm 4

THE CHARM OF

LINEAGE

89

*I*magine you are sitting at the base
of your tree. It is evening, and the
moon is rising in a misty blue sky.
Start to notice your feet and legs, their
contact with the earth.

Your senses reach out to taste, smell,
touch, hear, and feel the evening, and
you are very comfortable. Bark is
against your back but feels moulded to
your shape. Branches are above you;
deep within, you sense that the spirit of
the dryad is awake and content.

You have an instinct that you are in a timeless place; the cool air blowing, lifting your hair, lifting the leaves.

If the time was right, these sensations could transport you back to a time when you were tiny and all trees were giants. By comparison with today's trees, you are still very small, but that's fine: you are completely protected and supported by the earth, the air, and your tree.

Stretch your legs out or cuddle them to you. Think gently about where you have come from, focusing on positive images. Think about where the tree has come from; its tiny seed, shoot, and sapling through its growth to a mature tree. Think of your age and its age. You are just two living, growing intelligences whom life has brought together in this time and this place, sharing a quiet moment together.

Repeat this anytime you wish.

WE HAVE ESTABLISHED a link with a particular tree's dryad in our imaginal realm. I use this phrase to distinguish from "imagination," which has
been diminished in our culture to mean "make believe." The imaginal realm
signifies a place that is completely real in its own plane or realm. It is a potent
tool in creating our outlook, so we're going with the flow and seeing what
transpires. In fact, we're learning to relax and enjoy the forest party.

This latest charm concerns honouring our dryad's lineage. Trees are long
lived: not all we see are indigenous, but whatever their origins, they hold the
historic memory of that place and from where they now stand in your locality.
Every tree is a witness to all that has happened and understands the terrain
far better than we can. As well as their physical history, they are rooted deep
in the human psyche. Trees have been the subjects of myth, legend, and folklore since humans started telling stories. Ancient tales from all cultures insist
on the relationship between trees and humans, and we need to integrate that
idea. The trees and us are a great partnership for the good of both and the
world.

When we attune ourselves to become the charms that attract our dryads,
we also deepen our understanding of our relationships in the world in a very
positive way. Opening up to nature, our viewpoint is subtly but definitely
altered. We are brought back into a communion with the world, allowing our default position of "always humans first" gradually to change. We
arrive—often just for odd moments, then gradually more often and for longer periods—to a position of relationship. Eventually, our instinctive knowing emerges from the shadows and our perspective changes to one that is
healthier, more mature and helpful to us.

We begin to experience all life as inspirited in its own way. In a world
where speed, distance, and constant change dominate, spending time with
the trees, so rooted, calm, and long lived, is a healing antidote. These feelings

of earth connection and interrelationship are hardwired; they are what have inspired the most ancient myths and legends.

Our exciting challenge now is to meet our dryad in folklore and myth. The close study of our actual tree has been part of our focus on its spirit, the dryad, and its place in the landscape. The two are closely intertwined, and we must join them up in our minds. Now, we will look at its lineage and heritage, which will necessitate searches of all kinds. Students need knowledge, not just intuition, and love the insights which gentle study can bring.

We will start by finding out about our dryad's wider tree family. Is its tree indigenous or a specimen of imported variety? How many different varieties of tree are in the overarching family? Can you work out your tree's approximate age? You have been chosen by this tree and feel a relationship forming, so feel free to begin asking the dryad which stories they would like to tell you; you can share your own on your next few visits. Storytelling is a large part of our next phase of communication, so if you don't feel too confident in that department, read the section through thoroughly. You can then practice telling stories in meditation and dreaming before you go out.

Can you find any traditional evidence for a personality or spiritual quality attached to a species? An example from Iroquois legend tells us that a human messenger from Great Spirit called the Peacemaker was approached because of a period of cyclical conflict and endless bloody reprisal. He instructed that weapons be buried under the White Pine; that its needles grow in clusters of five to symbolise the five nations; that its roots spread out in the four directions as "peace roots"; that its branches grew wide to shelter all, and that an eagle would perch high above to watch over the roots.[7] No wonder it is regarded as the tree of peace, and such stories show us what an intrinsic part their physical characteristics and medical uses play in shaping their mythic stories.

It is only respectful to explore the legends of your dryad's tree. It is a labour of fascination, of love.

· · · · · · · · · · · · ·

7 See https://druidgarden.wordpress.com/tag/magic-of-pine/ for this story and the tree's history, uses, and ecology (accessed 20 October 2020).

Write a list in your journal the names of any trees you discover that our forebears thought were friendly, happy to help humans, giving of prophetic messages, surly, or taciturn.

If your tree wouldn't naturally grow in your country, discover the fun of researching the folklore of other cultures to find its associations. As you range through stories, everything will feed into knowing your dryad just a little better.

As well as discovering tree qualities (oak: steadfastness; hawthorn: fairy magic; holly: strength, and so on), we love their stories. From Northern Europe we have Snow White and the apple, Finn the Warrior and the hazel, holly and Sir Gawain and the Green Knight, the oak and the Druid, Frau Holle the Elder Mother, King Arthur and Avalon (Isle of Apples), Old Man Willow and Tom Bombadil, Merlin and Merlin's oak—and that's just scratching the surface. Every culture is rich in such examples, so range far and wide. Africa has a wealth of tree/goddess connections. From Asia, the Bodhi tree, the sacred fig, shaded Buddha as he attained enlightenment. The tree of life has too many forms to mention them all, and the living tree (or pole) is a symbol of Asherah and other goddesses of the Middle East. The ancient Sumerian goddess Inanna, in the Epic of Gilgamesh, planted the willow tree, the Huluppu tree, in a holy garden; elements of this story become part of the Adam and Eve legend. Wherever we look around the world, the sacred tree is there.

The Yoruba people of Nigeria have a valuable word, *orisha*, for nature spirits who interact with humans especially to help them live well on the earth. Human/tree communications are common in stories we have always told our children—there are far more forests than fairies in our fairy stories,[8] showing their significance. The ancient resonance of myth is often used in fantasy fiction, and much of it comes from Greek legends, where dryads were portrayed as beautiful nymphs of the trees. If, to you, the dryad is simply the inspirited

• • • • • • • • • • • •

8   Some examples are the forests of the Grimms' fairy tales and Red Riding Hood, Rumplestiltskin, and the Babes in the Wood; the Narnia stories of C. S. Lewis; the Faraway tree of Enid Blyton; Kipling's *Jungle Book*; the hundred-acre wood of A. A. Milne's Winnie the Pooh; J. K. Rowling's Forbidden Forest in the Harry Potter series; and J. R. R. Tolkien's forest of Middle Earth and its tree people, the Ents.

tree, then just enjoy the different interpretations below. They are all writers' attempts to describe the indescribable—evocative descriptions to feed our yearning for a nature relationship. Dryads in modern eco-fiction again symbolise a yearning for a relationship we would have if our world was more in balance. Do the following descriptions chime with your internal image of your own dryad? Why not draw an aspect of them in your journal now?

Pale birch-girls were tossing their heads, willow-women pushed back their hair from their brooding faces ... the queenly beeches stood still and adored ... shaggy oak-men, lean and melancholy elms, shock-headed hollies (dark themselves, but their wives all bright with berries) and gay rowans, all bowed and rose again, shouting ... in their various husky or creaking or wave-like voices.[9]

Richly robed in gorgeous finery, and richer still her beauty; such the beauty of the Naides (Naiads) and Dryades (Dryads), as we used to hear, walking the woodland ways.[10]

Although classical dryads are feminine, we no longer find a rigid insistence on rigid gender allocation necessary or helpful. If humans are increasingly unwilling to be classified, then why insist on it for dryads? Maybe your dryad is a hermaphrodite or anywhere along the spectrum that we understand as modern sexuality. In history, some are under the auspices of goddesses, and many dryads have a particular myth of their own.[11]

All this folklore fixes the idea firmly that the dryad is an entity rooted in folklore and the reality of our ancestors' lives, not a fairy of our own invention. And these stories are brilliant—real food for the inner person. We are building on a relationship enshrined in mythic history, a communion that has expressed itself as legend for aeons, whenever we visit our trees ... and it's nearly time to do that now.

Before we go outside, and especially if circumstances prevent you, we'll strengthen our dryad connection—counterintuitively by not doing anything, just by being together in the imaginal world in perfect safety and contentment. Make sure you are comfortable and free of distractions. On the screen behind your eyes is your imaginal forest. It is an inner world that has been awakening since you started this work. To evoke it, you might first look at images of trees or read a favourite tree poem, then read this through, close your eyes, and enter the green realm.

· · · · · · · · · · · · ·

9 C. S. Lewis, *Prince Caspian* (London: HarperCollins, 2009), 170.

10 A. D. Melville (trans.), *Ovid's Metamorphoses*, edited with introduction and notes by E. J. Kenney (Oxford: Oxford's World Classics, 2008), book VI, line 453.

11 See appendix 1 for a list of dryads from classical myth.

•MEDITATION•

Breathing with Your Dryad

Take a moment beneath the tree to *relaaaxxx*.

Breathe in the charged air, which comes from your tree's respiration and transpiration: water drawn from the roots travels to evaporate through the pores of its leaves. There is a constant flow, just as there is with you. Breathe with your tree; the water in your outbreath also evaporates. Your logical brain relaxes, knowing the benefits of forest bathing. Your subtler senses awaken.

Be open to immediate sounds and sensations—the temperature, scents, breezes, pigeons cooing. Allow your awareness to sink through those senses into a deeper awareness. The less-visible aspects of life open to your attention—the roots beneath you; the stones caught in the roots; the aura of the tree stretching beyond its canopy.

The centre of the tree trunk—the heartwood—is compacted: sense this strong column of past growth supporting the outer living fibres, which carry nourishment from roots to the highest tip. Feel the sun on the top of the high canopy, its energy being absorbed by the green chlorophyll in the leaves...

Sense the dryad in the life of the tree. Where are they today? Resting or awake? Deep within the trunk or dancing on the end of the boughs? Working or making wind-music with leaves and twigs? Stretching to the sun or pushing deep into the earth?

Be aware of going back and back, further than your tree, to its parent and grandparent. Each long-lived generation of trees has produced hundreds of seeds, shoots, new growth, new trees, and each life is so many years longer than ours. If you are happy to, drift back with your dryad to a land of forests, clear air, water, strange flora and fauna and dancing tree spirits. Dream the inspirited world, the myriad insects, butterflies, birds, foliage, and flowers.

Breathe with them all as if you also are growing through the action of wind, sun, and water.

Smile with fellow-feeling: your dryad is activating your green self, and you are reciprocating with attention and appreciation of their lineage.

Feel the moment passing and the need for your physical body to reassert itself and pick up your responsibilities. Smile again, knowing you can return anytime. Say thank you and consciously separate, turning away in your imagination and allowing the image to fade as you return to the known world.

· · · · · · · · ·

The energy of the feeling you generate from the meditation will flow ahead of you and your "dreamings" at home will prompt a response long before you ceremonially ask your tree for communion. Relax and trust that this will happen before you go to the trees.

At home or when walking, keep examining how you are interacting with the world of the tree spirits.

> *Always bear in mind that the*
> *physical world is physical and*
> *the imaginal is imaginal; we*
> *do not blur the boundaries.*

Each world has its own truth and reality, and they do not interact in physicality. Sci-fi and magical fiction are full of disastrous consequences of just this happening.[12] We respect and believe each in its own sphere, but, not being fantasists, we do not confuse the two.

So yes, our imaginal experiences are real in their own sphere. They are subjective and strong; they are experiences, so we do not doubt them; but we hold the truth of them in our sacred inner world. They become a part of our background understanding, a spiritual dimension that enriches and adds

· · · · · · · · · · · ·

12 Alan Garner, *Elidor* (London: CollinsVoyager, 2002), centring around
     the intrusion of the magical world into modern Manchester, is a
     terrifying case in point.

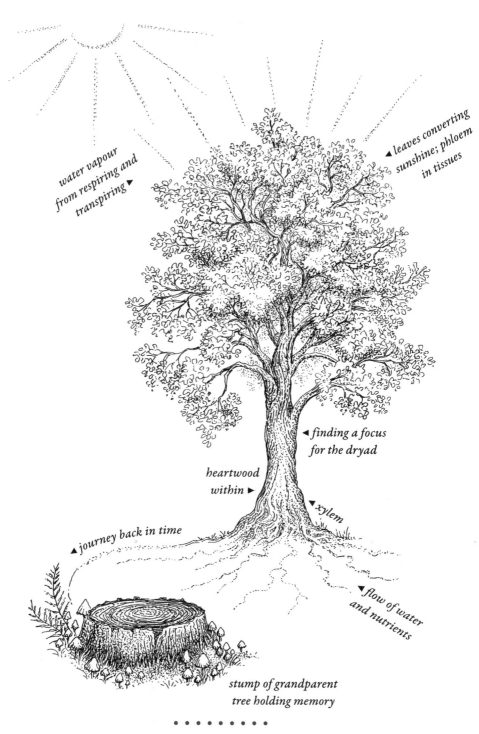

water vapour
from respiring and
transpiring ▼

▲ leaves converting
sunshine; phloem
in tissues

▲ finding a focus
for the dryad

heartwood
within ▶

▼ xylem

◀ journey back in time

▼ flow of water
and nutrients

stump of grandparent
tree holding memory

• • • • • • • • •

Tree Physicality and Lineage

depth and texture to the "real" world of the five senses. They colour the real life in which we are firmly embedded, obeying its laws and those of society.

And what next? The world of nature is calling you to go and visit your tree, to share some stories.

Here is your *aide-mémoire*:

Checklist for Going to Share Stories

○ Keep up the expectation of being fascinated, of going further, of learning more.

○ Keep visiting; keep talking and, above all, keep noticing.

○ When away from your tree, keep it in mind.

○ Send "good morning" and "good evening" to your dryad. Visit as often as you can.

○ Read books, herbals, folklore.

○ Then visit again.

○ Every time you find out something new from your research, make sure to tell your dryad; then be alert for any response.

○ When you visit, let it become a habit to share a story or a praise chant or poem or some news from your life; again, wait for any response.

○ As ever, begin exercises by saying hello and asking permission; end with thanks.

· · · · · · · · ·

To honour the charm of heritage and lineage, we are learning and lightly, subtly, relaxedly amplifying our ways of connection.

Each part of our threefold knowing of our dryad colours our relationship.

- ✻ Knowing our tree/dryad's physical presence
- ✻ Knowing their attributes and qualities
- ✻ Knowing what our dryad represents in tradition

Charm 4 Synopsis

✹ The fourth charm is generated by our respect and brings a gift from the forest: an expansion into our rootedness through the land and the lineage of our dryad.

✹ We become fascinated with the heritage of our dryad. The glamour of ancient myth and folkloric tales will flow from us to our tree as we use what we've read. We make friends by exchanging stories of our histories and lives. We are creating a magical interaction with our dryad.

Route Map for Charm 4

I honour the history and lineage of the trees and dryads; I research; I make, recount, and share story; I am still and imagine; I thank and withdraw; I note and record.

Applying Charm 4

Respecting Our Stories

*I am a repository of myth and
story; I go to the trees to share.*

THIS PRACTICAL SESSION is about considering and integrating, and it has three distinct phases.

We consider our dryad's physical/spiritual lineage in its present environment; consider the mythic lineage our dryad holds, regardless of the culture/environment they now live in; and we combine these through story.

The dryad's place in history and in the present world flows from us to our dryad; that is stage one.

Stage two, after telling the stories that emerge to the trees, is to allow the return flow. Those ideas from our minds will be influenced by the dryad's intuitive response. Being within its physical ambience and testing our stories right under their tree can be salutary: do they still feel "right"? Sometimes, in the comfort of our homes, we just go off on flights of fancy, which the reality of damp bark and dripping leaves will soon quash.

To formulate our stories to tell the dryads, if it feels right to do so, we can use the checklists further on: stories of our physical lineage, our various roles in the world, our family myths that have shaped our beings. But, as always, we are in charge; we choose. So, if we have distressing memories or no family or even if our own stories seem irrelevant, we need not revisit them. Our alternative is, what stories do we wish to tell? Choose those instead! Thus, we exchange tales as another joyful sharing to charm our dryad. The notes below invite us to be inventive storytellers, limited only by our imaginations, feeling light and liberated.

It's time to get the walking boots on for some more dryad visiting, enriched by our study of the trees' lineage. If you can't get out, something tangible will help to connect you to your dryad. Obtain from a neighbour or friend a bunch of twigs, some fir cones, acorns or other tree fruits, some bark fallen from a plane or pine, or leaves to dry, to add to what you have already collected around you. Have a nature table or shelf on or under which you can also store your work and research books. It will not raise eyebrows that anyone housebound appreciates seeing the beauty of nature in their home.

As usual, send your thoughts—this time on heritage and myth—ahead of you. As your tree appears, see imaginatively the energy whirls from your last dance together and the dryad peeping from the leaves. Send these thoughts:

* We share an energetic heritage to the landscape and the trees.

* Some of us "belong" historically; some have made a new relationship with this land.

* I/you were born here/moved here/am established/ am new/etc.

* All who live here are welcomed and belong.

* All bring their own gifts and stories to enrich this place. Let us share them.

So many of us move to new places and even continents these days, this is a useful mantra as we connect to nature, which so loves and expresses diversity.

This section is written as if it will all happen in one visit, but as there are a number of stages, little and often is the better way. It certainly grew to several sections as I explored it, and I still return to this charm and discover new things. Just remember to report in your journal at every stage.

Approaching, we notice the physicality of the landscape as an invitation to continue always to learn and explore our dryad's role in the landscape. And, when we arrive, we ask questions, exchange information through story and dream with myth and legend.

We've been walking: we're by our tree now. Settle comfortably at the roots or lean against it; you have a lot more thinking and imagining to come. Trust that you will attract no special attention and relax, feeling the tree's weight supporting you.

•EXERCISE•

Our Dryad Within the Tree

The dryad moves effortlessly around their domain, but here is one useful exercise in locating them. Settle down—with breathing, relaxing, dreaming, and greetings—into a rhythm that your dryad will recognise. Allow a feeling of good companionship to arise and send it to the tree. Sit or lean with your back to the tree and imagine the dryad as if, if you turned around, they would be revealed...

Traditionally, the dryad rests at the crutch of the lowest large branch and the trunk; see them there in your imagination.

Then slowly, as you would when glimpsing any other wild species, turn with semi-focused eyes. Gaze with soft eyes at the trunk—can you discern significant shapes in the bark? Eyes? Arms? A face? An expression? Most trees have myriad faces and attitudes, and will reveal two or three to you each time, so do not limit yourself; keep looking with an open mind each time you go.

Draw and make notes in your journal. Take as long as you like as you start to perceive the spirit within.

Does the ephemeral nature of your tree become clearer if you look beyond it? Step back from it and focus some metres beyond its silhouette. Can you see its aura? This is a recognised technique to help sense the energy of all living beings. Have no expectations, but trust what you see. For some lucky people, this may be colours and waves; for most of us, it is far more subtle than that, maybe a slight quiver, a middle ground of exuding energy that slightly thickens the air between tree and sky. Whilst you are in sensitised mode, look up into the canopy to see the glinting light, like blinking eyes, through the leaves.

You will feel when it's right to end the session. This work can be deeply involving, so take it at your own pace. Whenever you do finish, it's important to feel your own unique completeness, your separation from the tree, and, as ever, we use ritualised actions to ensure this.

Deliberately concentrate on your own energy field and assert it as a vibrant, complete, and whole egg shape. End with the thanks and farewell habit that is by now programmed into your brain.

Then stop outside the aura of the tree, feeling and affirming your smooth and unbroken energy field as being completely separate from that of the tree.

. . . .

Reread your notes on this exercise over the next weeks, and use the following extension exercise if and when it attracts you. It is an opportunity quietly to muse about the locality that has produced the landscape. Through generations, humans have worked hand in hand with nature, planting what would flourish: the legacy of the past is there, a living book to be read. What can you deduce? Answer each of the exercise's questions in your journal. Imaginative interpretation is the aim, not historical accuracy. If you wish, you can check your facts later.

Musing On History

Settle down as before. Tree myths, their physicality, qualities, and character-istics all blend together into our holistic appreciation. Although the ques-tions are practical, you might start by opening to a sense of the tree's—and the landscape's—aura: the fluid, moving energy field within which all sen-tient forms live. When you have a firm remembrance of this, dream with these questions:

- 🍁 What was this place like ten years ago? Twenty? Fifty? One hundred? When do you think your dryad's tree first pushed through the soil as a tender shoot here? Was it planted by humans?

- 🍁 Any tree's growth will tell you which trees like the soil and weather conditions and which are struggling; what do your eyes tell you?

- 🍁 Does your tree naturally grow fast or slowly? Is this part of your dryad's temperament?

- 🍁 How does your tree/dryad relate to its wider landscape? Is the species indigenous or imported? If its heritage is far away, how has it adapted? Does it have scars? How were they caused?

- 🍁 Is it larger, smaller, more robust, or more tender than the surrounding trees?

🍁 Almost all trees have been used by humans—for carving, for kitchenware, as fuel, as joists in houses. Find the particularity of your dryad's tree if you don't already know it. If you discover your birch dryad's wood makes implements for doctors, dentists, and chefs, does its clean astringency give you extra insight into your dryad's personality?

The exercise reminds us that an understanding of physicality does not detract from spirit but enhances it. Thank the whole landscape when you end.

• • • • • • • • • •

You may wish to ask questions. Is there a difference between asking in your imagination and asking out loud? Which concentrates your mind the best? Keep experimenting.

Your questions will drift down into the tree roots, up to the highest boughs, and to your dryad. Let each hang in the air before dispersing, and don't hurry the answer. Practice being open to the stirrings of a response. Intuit the answers in the rustling replies of the tree, and always filter through your common sense.

If no responses come, just go on to the next ... trust that they will answer in their own good time, and ask to recognise their answers when they do come—perhaps as breezes, feelings of cold or heat, sensing, intuitions, as dreams, as odd thoughts. Possible questions moving from the physical to the spiritual and back again might be:

🍁 Does your tree dryad have a particular role in its landscape?

🍁 Are they a guardian, a dancer, a warrior, a barrier, a far-seer, a dreamer, a witness, or something else?

🍁 Are they a protector of others—animals, birds, small shrubs, and plants—or are they protected by other species?

If you're not sure of anything, ask.

In fact, how will you know unless
you ask? You have all the time
in the world to learn more...

This can become one of several dreamy yet focused sessions during which you may feel your relationship reaches a new level. Jot down questions as they occur or write a list beforehand. There is so much information here that we need to keep clear what we're doing.

Compare this relationship again to a human friendship: when we share our circumstances and feelings, when we get to know others' lifestyles, the roles they inhabit, and how they relate to the world, we feel closer to them. We are beginning to understand them.

Remembering our relationship with the spirit of the trees is reciprocal. On a subsequent visit it will be your turn to share; you choose the time and, instead of questioning, you will be storytelling. You can do this simply by imagining your dryad asking you exactly the same questions that you asked them.

Why not explain the particular relationship between your physical size and temperament, your habits and the way you relate to your home and surroundings? We don't generally consider these things, and this can be a gentle way to explore, with the dryad as a nonjudgmental witness. If the time is not right, leave it. The trees feel no hurry. Trust always the barometer of your feelings.

When we observe how we relate to our landscape (city street or country vista) or our roles (parent, child, worker), we need many titles and differing qualities to fulfil them all. We may be tender but a protector; robust yet in need of nurture; a guardian needing time to be a dreamer. Every human is as fascinating as each dryad, but we take ourselves for granted; without ever considering, we think we understand ourselves.

Storytelling is a great connection between people of all species, so before you leave this charm, tell your dryad at least one story with a beginning, middle, and end. Have you ever told a story out loud? Storytelling can seem intimidating, but it is freeing and can really open up channels of communication. Welcome, storyteller, to your new role! From fairy tales you have a tried and tested opening to start with, for traditional openings formalise and create distance, establishing the story as separate to us and making a safe space in which we can share.

· · · · · · · · ·

Making Story

Try inserting your name after these openings, and notice how it feels to put yourself into the opening of a story. Try it now, reading aloud and finishing each sentence:

Once upon a time, [your name]…

A long ago in a distant place, [your name]…

If you or your dryad are new to the area, try:

*In a place far from here, [your name] went
adventuring to a new land…*

Or why not play with these evocative openings from other cultures?
From West Africa:

*Long ago, when a tiny child could still understand
the voice of the wind in the trees…*

A story, a story; let it come, let it go…

Or from the Navajo tradition:

*At the time when men and animals were all
the same and spoke the same language…*

These openings strike just the right chord for our dryad connection, assuming as they do an interspecies connection to the world. Make up your own.

*Back in the world when [insert something you believed
as a child: when my dog sang to me, when my steps
made the crunchy snow say ouch, and so on].*

If you can't think of any memories, then invent! If you don't want to share your actual story, then just don't; no ifs or buts.

But that doesn't stop you from sharing a story: just invent wildly, joyously, outrageously, for your fun and that of your dryad.

> *Once, when the rivers ran like sparkling lemonade*
> *and the gingerbread houses were rented out to friendly*
> *fairies, [your name] took a trail into the woods…*

> *One night, in a time when small children could still*
> *hear the music of the spheres, a shooting star sped*
> *toward [your name's] bedroom window…*

How to finish? Well, that's where we need to deviate from our traditional tales. We don't want a neat finish, as our life is ongoing. "Happily ever after" is static, and we want to keep fluid and flowing with our dryad, so we need to make up our own ending, perhaps inventing a formal phrase just for ourselves:

> *And [your name] lived on happily; always*
> *looking out for the next joyous adventure.*

· · · · · · · · · ·

That's a lot of instruction—just start, and see where your story leads you. Chat; engage; allow your imagination free rein. Your fascination will lead you.

> *To charm, we respect the history*
> *of our dryad. We add to an*
> *ancient and living tradition*
> *by sharing our own stories.*

Q: Why rearrange our relationships with the world?

A: Because we need a clear sense of self to embrace life fully.

Charm 5

THE CHARM OF

RIGHT RELATIONSHIP

*I*n your imagination, prepare to
leave the house. You will soon be
walking, and rootedness flows through
you. As you don your coat, cloak
yourself with intention, your head in
the clouds: airy energy suffuses you.
Like an ambulant tree, earth and sky
meet within you as you walk to the
threshold and your perception shifts...

In your mind's eye, you look down from a bird's perspective, seeing yourself as a dot surrounded by a circle of your aura, the sphere of your influence, and your horizon; it is also the astronomical sign for the Sun (☉). The energetic field is permeable but can be strengthened or made more fluid by intention.

Your quality of upright centredness is echoed in your dryad as you meet in mutual strength and respect.

WE ARE ALWAYS the centre of our universe and can always access the still centre of our being. When we have practiced noticing and remembering this, we go further to notice and respect it in all other life forms, starting with our tree and its dryad. These exercises in noticing have distinct geometrical forms.

Turn around on the spot, now, wherever you are (or in imagination if you are chair-bound). Your senses are delineating your own horizon. Primarily we use our visual sense, but hearing, tasting, smelling, and touching all play their part, so shut your eyes to amplify these.

> *Get a real sense of being centred*
> *in your own space. Does it please*
> *you? Is it physically clear? If*
> *not, alter what you need to.*

As you walk toward your tree, its dryad will be on the periphery of your sphere. The dryad also has its own circle, and as you approach it, you will be simultaneously centred in your own and on the edge of the dryad's. Walking will close that distance until you stand together as near as you can get to the two circles overlapping exactly: they in theirs, you in yours. Whilst there, you will mutually allow your energies to abut and then meld for a brief time.

This is what we habitually allow with our family and loved ones. That relationship is shown as the Venn diagram of mathematics, which sacred geometry calls the vesica piscis. It has myriad symbolic meanings, and its midpoint is the place of meeting, of held sharing and experience: ⦾.

We can separate what we're doing into steps:

* We each consciously become aware of our centrality in our space.

* We become clear on setting boundaries so that we can engage and disengage each time.

* Then we allow fluid interaction and withdrawal by our will and intent.

In this way we can grow our connection with our dryad, using parameters of two-way equality and respect.

Considering our boundaries will also positively impact our everyday life. So many social boundaries have disappeared in the last twenty years that it is good to review our human interactions. This puts the onus on us to exercise personal responsibility in maintaining those that we need. Consciously doing this encourages an appropriate flow in communion with all aspects of the natural world. If we practice being the upright, bridging heart of our universe, we can maintain that position whilst our living becomes harmonious movement into a constantly fluid set of relationships. This counteracts the fixed, immutable vision of self and world that keeps us stuck far from enchantment. So we're preparing to embrace a different perspective taking overlapping relationships into account.

Seeing the trees, rivers, stones, and footpaths each also centred in their own space presents the world as a series of possible communications through overlaying energies. We can extend out to many liminal points. We can become intrigued by the notion of these places of transition; we need to investigate how they feel and what might happen.

The idea brings a whiff of enchanted possibility into our lives. Activate this feeling to be open to magic.

The Vesica Piscis

In your imaginal space, in the comfort of your own home, sit with your tree and its dryad, your inner senses activated, and be gentle and patient. Dryads are hidden beings; this is a trust exercise on both sides. If you wish, take off your shoes, close your eyes, and become one with the space. Assert that you are safe and in charge, always, and that you will receive only what you are ready for and give only what you are happy to. Feel free to stop at any time if you are at all unsure.

Feel yourself merging with the soft air that flows through you, and feel your still centre strongly. Allow that centre to expand into a large energetic globe all around you, having height, depth, and circumference. When that is established, sense a similar globe extending from the centre of your dryad-in-residence. If it feels right, gently move into the central intersection of the two globes to meet your dryad. Sense that they are respectfully allowing you to acclimatise and following your lead: you are thankful for their gracious gentleness, for you feel their potency. Relax. Just being together in the space may be enough for now.

The effect of meeting your dryad may be to deepen you into hearing with different ears, seeing with different eyes. This great breathing entity has changed the atmosphere within which you are breathing. This space is greener and cooler than its surroundings, and the air is fresher. Do not send your senses out to gain impressions; you have all that you need in this protected space, so allow the impressions to drift into you. In your imagination you are filled with the landscape. You are an intrinsic part of the green, the source of your refreshment. Feel the connection between your spine and the trunk of the tree: both upright, both with life flowing through them. The life force flows through you both: in this you are family.

Allow plenty of time and come back slowly, feeling yourself wholly and completely separated from your tree at the end. This is good practice and prepares you for deeper work with your actual tree.

> *Most of us rush out of the ending of*
> *a meditation. Be always slow and*
> *gradual, and notice your impressions*
> *as you move from your inner to outer*
> *awareness; it is another magical cusp*
> *point before our final arrival back*
> *to our own vibrant completeness.*

As we look now at personality and rhythm, we need another of our moments of consideration. We naturally interpret the dryad's reactions to us in a "humanising" way. Our brains will translate feelings we receive into phrases. It's our way of making sense of a new way of communicating, but we should not anthropomorphise. A dryad is not a human and has completely different motivations and understanding of life, which will always be mysterious to us. They obey their own laws of nature, so a tree with a falling rotten branch may still kill us. The concepts of friendliness, family, and understanding are all exclusive consciously to humans—as far as we know; and though each inhabitant of the tree kingdom seems to show these qualities through their actions to their fellow trees, we are wise not to rely on interspecies exhibitions of such emotions.

It is only through the imaginal world that we gain an inkling of how to communicate, and with a limited vocabulary, many of us having only practiced heretofore with other humans. Confirmed pet lovers have the advantage here. Some trees appear to be unfailingly generous or healing or delightful, cheery company. Others may seem weak or indifferent to us, or subject to "moods," and we trust these instincts and perceptions. It is easy for us to be "spooked" by a tree's power; again, we trust our intuition. Hold all lightly. We are students, and knowing how little we know keeps us open to new lessons.

It is possible that a "reserved" tree has chosen you. With respect and patience, your understanding can be as deep as with a more open-seeming personality. We value what we have to work for. Every tree, every dryad, has something to offer—a unique quality, just as every human has—and the lesson may well be the wisdom of keeping our distance. But from most there is the possibility of a supportive energy and a wider viewpoint.

Learning the rhythm of our dryad is a part of learning its personality—or, if that is too anthropomorphic, its energetic quality. When is its most active period? When is it at its sleepiest? The dryad's life is hidden, so "tune in" at liminal times, dawn and dusk, when the worlds are at their most permeable. This is a big job that will continue throughout the year and at all times of day. So put the book down and tune into your dryad now: How awake is it? How responsive? Say hello from wherever you are. Intuit the response; write it and the time in your journal.

Researchers have monitored the telluric (earth) currents at sacred sites and found magnetic and radiation anomalies particularly at dawn and dusk, and high incidents of "unidentified atmospheric phenomena."[13] These findings are highly cogent, as we are concerned with our instinctive responses and if it is easier to communicate at certain times, that is vital information.

> *Our delight will be in discovering*
> *more about our dryad's rhythms.*

. . . .

13 The Dragon Project Trust: Researches into rumours about the power and properties of ancient sacred sites, which started c. 1977, is a well-documented example of this type of work. For their extensive findings, go to http://www.dragonprojecttrust.org/research (accessed June 2020).

Checklist of the Dryad's Rhythm

The dryad's rhythm—is it

- ○ a morning, afternoon, evening, or night being?

- ○ especially attractive to birds at particular times?

- ○ more dormant in winter?

- ○ changing in aura as it powers down for the fall of the leaves?

- ○ bursting with energy at the spring rising of the sap?

- ○ favouring a particular time for display, for attracting attention?

· · · · · · · · ·

We have to watch carefully for the display, which can occur at any time: it may not be when we expect. I remember distinctly the show of green acorns on a stand of oaks long before I was expecting them, in a dark wood. They were green jewels, a gift from the dryad. And we might automatically associate the holly's display time with red berries—until becoming transfixed by their small white summer flowers for the first time. Year by year, our perceptions change: our noticing and perceptions remain fluid.

> *Once we think "I know," we*
> *have become rigid, and that*
> *cuts off communication.*

We are looking at auras of green energy, although they are often not a clear hue. There is a word for that magical colour; Brythonic (early British) language called it "glas"—interpreted as blue, grey, or grey-green but also glass-like. Glass itself is mysterious, being an amorphous solid, somewhere between liquid and solid matter, so it is fun to see a connection between that and our tree's aura. How does it fluctuate? How can you monitor and honour that? When will you dance with your dryad and when sing them a lullaby?

You may also consider the differences in rhythm between the tree spirits of deciduous and evergreens, and will have realised that suiting your dryad's routine rather than your own preferences is becoming inevitable. How can you adapt to fully exploring your dryad's life through the seasons? Just do your best and trust that that will be sufficient for now. Visit at as many differing times of day and season as you can to share their quiet, active, studious, and merry moods. Keep checking in, and that extra effort of being aware or visiting when you are tired or rushed, to suit your dryad, will surely be appreciated. When common sense tells you to stay in for mobility, safety, or any other concerns, go in your imagination.

Speaking only from my own experience, the ethos of sincerity and wish to act "for the good of all beings" is a good prompt to the natural world to look kindly on your actions.

Where you cannot visit often, you must tune in at a distance to maintain a relationship. Hopefully you have an image or a token gift from your tree; use this as a focus to activate your bond. If you haven't yet felt the instinct to pick up a twig, seed, or leaf, then ask next time you visit. Don't ignore a genuine offering by holding out for a mystical Hollywood experience. A film-worthy bolt of lightning is rare—fortunately, as it might kill you—but a simple sycamore or ash key on the ground can be a potent gift and especial fun when thrown down onto your head by a squirrel.

Once gained, try sleeping with it under your pillow, setting the intent that it will be a passport and talisman for you to visit the world of the dryads. Keep your journal by the side of your bed to write down any impressions the second you awaken. How does your dryad appear in dreams? What landscape do they inhabit in your inner world?

Suppose we could actually look through the eyes of the dryad? How wonderful would it be to be nourished directly from the air, the earth, the rain, the sun, moon, and stars? Well, we all are, of course. Our lives rely on the constant interweaving planetary influences. The weather allows the continuity of life in your region. Without air and water we would die; the sun is vital for vitamin D absorption and to ripen the crops that feed us, and so on.

Now, focus your attention on these things as if they are simple, understood, internal truths:

- ❧ A more spiritual nourishment from these sources is literally vital for a full life.

- ❧ The sun is pouring heat and vitality straight into our bones.

- ❧ The moon is expanding our imagination.

- ❧ Pure rain, spume, and mist are being absorbed directly through our skin.

Never mind the science; just suppose you were a tree spirit, a dryad. Would you hunch against the rain or turn your leaves to it? Shiver in the wind or dance with it? We do not have chlorophyll to process the sun or xylem and phloem [14] to transport water and nutrients, but we do have a will that can attune us back into our animal bodies and an imagination to absorb the benefits of the natural world, wherever we find ourselves.

Electricity makes night into day and changes winter temperatures into those of summer in our homes, but our bodies and minds are still Stone Age, relating to the rhythm of the seasons. We hold a template of interconnection deep within us, which prompts an ancient imperative to in/action according to the season, amount of light, temperature, and so on.

Connecting to our dryad helps to awaken this dormant sense of right relationship with the seasons. Our dryad might just be the first step to coming into communion with the whole sentient world!

. . . .

14 These are the tissues that transport food around the tree: xylem moves water and dissolved minerals up from the roots; phloem moves sucrose from where it is produced in the leaves to other living parts—roots, shoots, and seeds.

Charm 5 Synopsis

❦ Generated by looking outward from a strong centre and allowing flow, charm 5 brings a gift from the forest: access to more communication with the natural world than we ever could have imagined!

❦ We move fluidly, maintaining a strong centre and looking constantly to the horizon, to willingly change our perspective for a while. We

allow gifts to flow both ways, welcome them, and trust our sincere feeling: "I long to get into right relationship with the world."

Route Map for Charm 5

I pause; I centre; I notice my horizon;
I switch perspectives at will; I notice and am noticed;
I exchange viewpoints; I thank and withdraw;
I note and record.

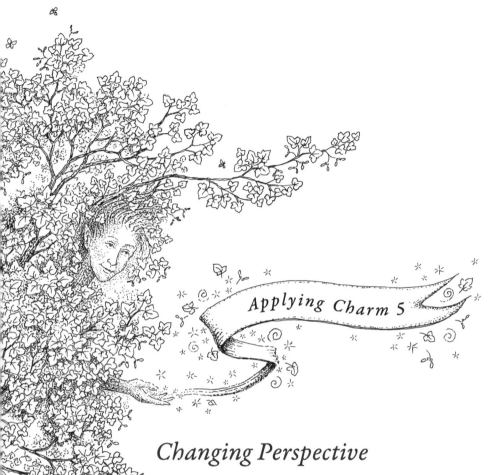

Applying Charm 5

Changing Perspective

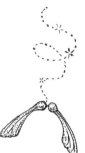

I am both firm and flowing,
holding the sense of lightness
and joy deep within.

THIS CHARM WILL help to consolidate our ability to check in with our dryad when we're out and about, become more adept at sensing their auras, and change our perspective to develop that sensibility still further.

Our standard form of "asking permission" may now change subtly. It is a permanent place in our resource kit, especially when exploring new terrain and meeting strange trees, but, in a known environment, you may trust for what is appropriate at each greeting, as long as you still ask in some form. As with a human friend, we sense the line of communication to take each time we get in touch, but we don't ignore the niceties. If we get it wrong, the friend, or the tree, will let us know—and even a friendly hazel dryad can deliver a stinging slap with a wet branch. If your phrase no longer feels fresh, then change it.

As you prepare for a walk, here is a swift foretaste of the next walking exercise to tune you in. If you wish, read it through in a meditative state.

Imagine a bird's eye view, focusing on the landscape from above, with yourself as the dot in the middle. Your greetings are effective from ever greater distances: send them ahead and assert your parameters and boundaries. You are a perfect essence of yourself. Feel into your auric field and sense its edge, lined with bright light, reflecting back any negative influences, leaving you clear within. You can also allow it to thin, as we do when a loved one comes near.

*Set it to "outside" mode, where you
feel prepared to encounter the world
of the unexpected: it is firm from
other outside influences but reaches
out to your dryad as you walk.*

*When do you notice your dryad's tree's
energy imprint? When does a tendril
of your energy meet that of the dryad?
As the tree comes within our horizon
and then ever nearer, these fields can
begin to meld if we wish and allow it.
Person and tree: each maintains their
strong centre. Activate that sense of
your inviolable core essence and hold
a gentle, fascinated, and questioning
attitude to how energies might meet
whilst maintaining the integrity of both.*

This should prepare you for your actual walk. Discard or amend anything that doesn't feel right to you as you put this imaginal adventure into practice.

Sharing Space with Our Dryad

As you walk, feel your centre and circumference. Pause frequently to change focus and see the scene also with the eyes of a hovering bird.

From this elevation, sense the animated lines of the vesica piscis symbol made up of your circular horizon and the dryad's shimmering around you both, changing fluidly as you get nearer. Stop frequently, allow time; this can be a powerful experience. The perspective-changing nature of this introduction helps you to move fluidly at will, but do take it gently.

If you are happy with each stage when approaching, sense a thinning in the boundary until the lines overlap and your two circumferences become a centre lozenge. You will both be safely enclosed yet still separate entities in the centre. Sketch this in your journal at some point.

Take time to imagine your aura reaching out lovingly, questioningly. Your inner eyes sense the dryad moving sinuously within their trunk or see the tree as inspirited, its life strong and flowing, in the way that is right for you.

You have already looked speculatively at your tree to detect its lines, its limbs, the hints of a dryad image imprinted on its physical reality. Now go through your imagined images to the life spirit of the tree.

Sit quietly by your tree and allow your senses full rein whilst within its aura. What does this evoke within you? How do your impressions compare with the exercise you did at home? When you are physically next to their tree, is your perception of your dryad different? Does it feel more truthful, more grounded?

Ask your dryad how best to communicate: how to stay aware of them. How will their messages come?

Person/Tree Meeting in Vesica Piscis

Every walk, wherever you go, is an opportunity to play with this session's ideas. In town, country, at work, or at leisure, you can imagine the flowing geometry of connection in the landscape—ellipses, lozenges, ovals, wave patterns. As you walk, can you pinpoint when you seem actually to be at a central place? Some landscapes help—in the centre of Stonehenge, within a perfect flat circle of the horizon, it is easy to feel at the centre of the universe. My homelier example is walking diagonally until at the centre of my local park. Lime trees border its four sides. From this central point, golden energy lines ray out to the four corners and sweep round to join up, making a magical circle of grass within which I may see wonders. I stand in the middle, my straightness connecting the heights and the depths, my feet rooting into earth and my arms stretching like high boughs to dance with the trees, for my influence, like that of the dryad, is actually in three dimensions, flowing up, down, and all around me, focused in whichever way I choose. I bend my attention toward my special dryad, sending a high arc toward the top of their tree, and see a breeze dipping their long boughs and twigs as if in response. I point my toes as I walk, allowing flashes of intent to reach toward the plane tree avenue I'm approaching, and imagine their aged dryads stirring. All this can happen in a few seconds and is part of an adaptable personal micro ritual, unobserved by others but priming me to see wonders in its wake: breeze and birds frequently supply the wonders.

Dryads are presented traditionally as nymphs, but do not have that expectation; we discussed earlier times and their different attitude to gender fluidity. You might have the impression that a holly or ash dryad is a warrior of indeterminate gender or your alder dryad is a deep-dreaming, gigantic, and supportive mentor beyond classification. The eight boughs of the hornbeam may be its many arms, the burr on the beech tree its bosom, the high circlet of evergreen leaves may crown a hermaphrodite figure with no limbs and just one eye staring from the bark. What wonderful creatures these wood spirits; how free to express the essence of their tree! Love each for what it is, without needing to turn it into a figment of your romantic imagination.

Trees have their own personalities, so you found one with whom you could share a mutual understanding. Now you can fine-tune exactly why. You will have noticed several aspects of your dryad: a face on one side, another mouth under a bough, an eye high above in a topmost bough. The tree's form in its trunk and bark is more fixed than our mobile skin and faces, but they have a way of showing us more than one temperamental face. All living beings are nuanced and can seem quixotic. Be fascinated to discover the changing aspects of your dryad that make it unlike any other. We all want to be valued for our uniqueness.

> *If you're always grumpy in the*
> *morning, then allow all sentient*
> *life forms to have their off times*
> *as well and be prepared to see a*
> *scowl emerging from a trunk.*

It is magical how differing aspects present themselves from such solid forms. The dryad who has been leaning out of my local holm oak is currently spookily lifelike, but on any day I might pass and find that it seems to have withdrawn back into its tree. I have observed this sort of change so often that I just accept it as a mysterious fact of life that might be in response to my needs, the season, or a combination of many other factors.

• EXERCISE •

Sympathetic Connection

Sit comfortably in your usual place under your tree.

Imagine the dryad deep within the tree, spreading their arms high above you along the lower branches. They might be stretching and dancing within the trunk. They might sing to you in the music of sky and air. They might be stretching high to the sun, sinewy legs delineated in the curving bark. Their shape need not follow the human pattern; they need not seem gendered; just allow a sense of a life form, a spirit, to arise. That is enough; trust your finer senses.

Draw them now whilst in your inner/outer place of consciousness.

Greet Your Dryad

What is your sense of them? Is this the right time? How do they feel on this occasion?

If they seem sleepy, if communication isn't easy, ask if you may just sit quietly with them; listen for the answer. If you sense it's okay, you can just enjoy relaxing there.

When you have a positive response from your dryad, then settle into contentment and ask for an insight into the world through their eyes. You may use the druid phrase, asking for connection "for the good of all beings," which will remind you of your spiritual ethos. Absorb impressions without thinking about them.

🍁 Ask what the world looks like from their perspective.

🍁 Enter the inner and deeper green ...

🍁 Trust in your own identity and allow yourself briefly to meld with the tree.

> *Enjoy five minutes of being long-lived*
> *and carefree—of fitting in perfectly.*

When you are ready, withdraw from your tree connection to activate your flying-bird viewpoint again, looking down from the tree's canopy.

From that height, you can revolve 360 degrees to greet the landscape to the horizon.

See flowing lines of green energy holding and enmeshing all aspects of the landscape. Your natural life force means that this is how you also are connected to it all.

Look across to the green between the trees. A flicker of vibrance and thickening of the atmosphere hints that your dryad is emerging to dance on the grass. Breathe an invitation to other dryads to come and join in. Hum gently to provide their soundtrack, and watch their revels. Again, no expectations. We cannot predict their form or movements, and must be open to appreciate what actually happens—perhaps a sandstorm-like whirl of energy. As the wind wafts, it aids the energetic movement from one tree to the next, expressing visually what the wind is doing, as a cornfield does. From the heights, see the patterns they make.

Next, will they allow you into the mystery of their rootedness? Will you learn about the relationship between root and fungus as a communicator? Is your dryad in communication with their neighbouring trees? How far do their roots extend? Do they touch, interlace with others? Just allow questions to arise and notice your response.

Delve deep into the roots—draw nourishment up. Feel it rising from the soles of your feet, and out through your head and upstretched arms. Then finish, completely and properly.

· · · · · · · · ·

This can be a real refreshment, remembered later to brighten a dull or painful time, or to help you drift off to sleep.

• • • • • • • • • •

Tree contact is nurturing and sustaining: we can feel reluctant to leave. If you love these exercises and know you'll be disinclined to separate and finish your session, go through the finishing guidelines once again.

Checklist for Disengaging from Your Tree Connection

○ Set a deliberate cutoff point for ending your visit beforehand. Set your phone alarm if you wish.

○ On leaving, walk beyond the tree's aura, turn to face and thank your dryad formally, and make a gesture of finality.

○ Reverse what you did at the beginning, finishing by seeing yourself as a point of essential essence, with your energy field intact.

○ Give a small gift (which can be as easy as noticing, carrying, and delivering to your tree whatever natural object takes your eye—a feather, a stone).

○ Touch the earth with your palms to ground yourself.

○ Walk away with finality, with your feet printing "thank you" on the soil.

> *Just because something happens*
> *in the realms of the imagination,*
> *never make the mistake of thinking*
> *that it is not real on its own*
> *plane. Treat it with respect.*

After this raft of experiences, it is wise to return at differing times, as suggested in charm 5. It demands an extra commitment to go to our tree when it's not so convenient: when we're cold or tired or it means missing a programme or getting up half an hour earlier. But in terms of particularity, it is very important. The evening or morning light, the dawn wind, or the silhouette of our tree under the stars gives us a whole new aspect. What does your dryad look like when their trunk is silvered by the full moon? When the shadow of a bush seems to be creeping toward them? When they appear gradually out of a thick fog or sparkle in the mist that heralds a hot day? Are they inviting you to return at these times in imagination at least, to meditate one day soon?

As always, only do what is safe and sensible. There is no possibility of intuitive work if you are concerned for your safety, so taking chances is counterproductive. Bookmark this charm to remind you to return to these exercises regularly through the year as well.

What will your dryad teach
you in the differing seasons?

Recording Experience

In recording this adventure, be precise with your experiences. Do not slip into generalities; we harnessed our fascination by focusing on specifics and particularities, for therein lies the magic. We are motivated by the highest feelings of love and may find our contact with the dryad intimate; their sense of grace and beauty can make contact with these beings sensual. Translate these feelings into the language you need: your responses are highly subjective, and your interpretations will relate directly back to what is personally relevant. In the imaginative realms, lines of communication are not all one way. We have invited and are making time for another sentient being to make a link with us, but hold all lightly—the theme to this book, and for a reason! We cannot dismiss our subjective viewpoint entirely, and our interpretations are limited by our current understanding and abilities. Do these exercises in a year's time and you will doubtless have a totally different experience. As our human/dryad relationship develops, we will find our witnessing awareness encouraging us into a larger understanding.

To charm, we reach out joyfully from a strong centre to flow imaginatively with the life of our dryad. May we be enriched by our varying viewpoints.

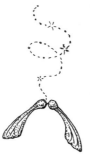

Q: How does asking dryads for a soul cure charm them?
A: We are all charmed to be appreciated for our talents, and the trees are great healers.

Charm 6

THE CHARM OF

HEALING

139

Now, in your mind's eye, you are taking an effortless journey to your tree. The restrictions of your body fade into the background for a few minutes as you evoke the joy of meeting your dryad again.

Hug your tree, each inbreath allowing any aches to flow down through the soles of your feet into the roots and the earth. Feel that any pain

can dissolve out from your heart space into the trunk, and all tension in your head is gently pulled into the high boughs, to be evaporated in the sun's rays.

Imagine your dryad absorbing and transforming all within them into pure neutral energy to be used by the living world.

Stay aware of being revitalised as you continue your day.

THERE IS A charm in being healthy, as far as we can. But, before you shut the book in despair, read on ...

The person glowing with life energy and focus attracts us and other life forms, but that person is not necessarily the most physically healthy, robust, strong, or energetic. Even in the dying, if the person holds a strong and authentic spirit, we can sense that charismatic attraction of the pure essence. I was told by an experienced therapist that clients divided themselves into youthful or elderly almost entirely by attitude to life, regardless of chronological age or state of health. The optimistic and enquiring, open to change and growth, still had a youthful energy and attractiveness: their physical limitations were less important to themselves than their interest in life. Those who presented as "old" were rigid and unwilling or unable to shift the opinions they'd formed earlier in life, even in their own best interests. One section looked outward and adapted so that their responses were appropriate to changing circumstances; the other looked inward to a reality that existed in their imaginations. The second type often doesn't see their attitude as a choice they can make at any time, but it really is. What will attract our dryad?

Evoking fascination regularly
helps us glow with youthful,
investigative energy: Where will
the adventure next take us?

So whatever the state of our physical selves, we can be young and healthy in our thinking. We just have to maintain that focus.

Looking outward and feeling it chiming with our internal truth, taking responsibility for our attitudes, we turn to our dryad for support and healing energy when we need it. And here is the caveat to the charm: bargains are reciprocal, and each side must benefit. Our part of the bargain is to aid the healing of the natural world in any practical way we can—supporting the right causes, bothering to write the letters, protecting our local environments against crude developers. To love a dryad is to understand the interdependence of all life forms and care for all nature in its multifarious forms. To care for another is the ultimate charm.

Take your time with this next visualisation. Observing the opening and closing rituals we've developed, we will visit a healing grove.

•VISUALISATION•

The Healing Grove

In imagination, you are walking through a park until you are standing in the middle of a grove of old trees, and you slowly turn to each. The first is an apple; ask what healing it brings, and the breeze whispers the answer to you ... *regeneration and magic.* Pause to receive it. Turn to the rowan and ask again, and the answer comes: *protection* ... Pause again. And then to an oak ... *strength* ... it flows around you, and together regeneration, protection, and strength settle on your shoulders like a cloak, soft and supportive. Snug in its soft warmth, allow yourself to drift as the antic breeze stirs the other trees and their influences begin to flow from them, whirling around you now too swiftly for you to identify. You sense their gifts of restoration, vitality, sovereignty, cleansing, joy, enlivening, perseverance, courage ... Each colours the air a different shade of green, gold, russet, and brown, every colour of nature, and you are the focus, bridging earth and sky in the middle, clothed in a cloak of brightness that they are weaving around you, absorbing exactly what you need. Relax for a long moment, a still centre of energy, glowing and beautiful.

And suddenly the air is still and the trees pull back into themselves. You thank them, lit up with the experience, and bring their blessings back, feeling fully present again in the world.

• • • • • • • • • •

This visualisation touches on the healing qualities of various trees that are largely accepted by tradition and research—and you will add to that your own practical findings. At any time, you can meditate and focus on the particular healing of one particular tree. As dryad charmers we already know that the trees' presence is health-giving. Now we turn our attention to the specific ways that they can help us.

Conventional Medicine

I have a deep respect for the wonders of conventional allopathic medicine, yet all health professionals acknowledge that healing remains a mysterious process. Nature's pharmacy is our ancestral birthright, and the drug industry makes good use of the active properties of many trees. The protection of the rainforests is vital partly because of the new remedies its plants might hold. Trees supply drugs, from the ubiquitous aspirin (willow) to new cancer treatments derived from yew and mistletoe.

Q: How and why do/don't people heal?

A: No one knows, but adopting a holistic approach
can only help us. Physical, mental, emotional, and spiritual
health intertwine, and the world of nature plays a vital
role in nourishing them all. Hospitals and hospices have
garden spaces and views of trees, for green space is a proven
health aid, as anyone immobilised by illness or injury will
attest. Hospitals also now attend to our emotional and
spiritual needs (although they might not express it in this
way) by using visualisation techniques, with strong trees a
favourite in supporting and absorbing a patient's pain.[15]

Traditional healing has much to say on the transference of pain, so doing this meditatively echoes folk beliefs and the customs of sympathetic magic. "Clootie trees" are an example, echoing the age-old habit of pilgrimage to trees growing by sacred waters. A clootie—a (natural fibre) rag of cloth—was dipped in the water and tied to the tree whilst asking the spirits for healing; as the cloth disintegrated, so the illness went from the body. This references the earliest of Celtic ritual acts, of casting votive offerings (often precious

. . . .

15 See https://www.beaumont.org/health-wellness/blogs/managing
-chronic-pain-through-guided-imagery, July 28, 2017 (accessed June
2020).

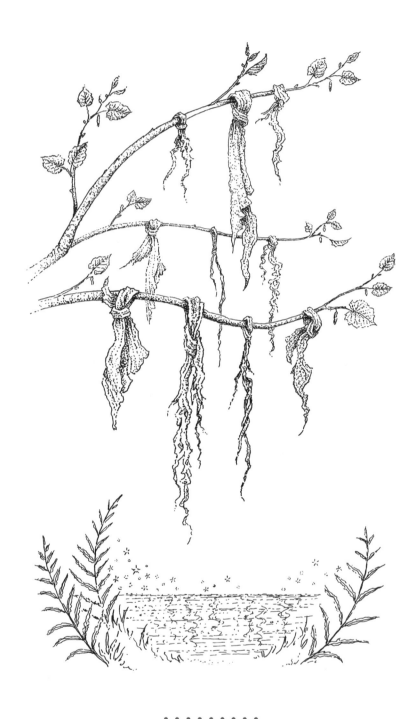

Clootie Tree

metal) into deep water, which we still do whenever we toss a silver coin into water, from the tackiest wishing well to the grandeur of the Trevi Fountain in Rome.

Using the underlying principle of trees "taking" an ailment, ash trees were used for toothache—alleviated by driving a nail into the tooth, then hammering the nail into its bark—and warts were pricked with a pin that was stuck in the tree with the rhyme, "Ashen tree, ashen tree, pray buy these warts from me." The old healing rhymes are easily overlooked but are actually very important. Many still exist in all cultures as messages from our forebears' more connected worldview.

Here's a possible reason for rhymes: as healing had to engage all the realms, all the helpers, the rhyme acted as a bridge to the otherworld. It is through this contact and help that the ill person would come back into right relationship, and health would result. This is a good encouragement to use rhyme when we next go to meet our dryad.

Rhymes, blessings, and charms to accompany all household tasks were collected between the 1860s–1900s from the Gaelic-speaking peoples of Scotland; the *Carmina Gadelica* is a compendium that whispers tantalisingly of a culture preserved in remote places up to very recent times.[16]

With traditional remedies, forgotten beliefs and medicine meet: trees have been used as literal portals to good health—physical "stepping or passing through" places. We found a portal to help us focus in the first charm, and we can extend this to healing doorways on our next outing. Take a break from reading now to make a list of any traditional rhymes—tree remedies, folk beliefs, superstitions, or weather indicators—you remember. Think back to childhood and local sayings that relate us back to nature. From the UK, with constantly changing weather, we have "Oak's before the ash, we're in for a splash; ash before the oak, in for a soak" and "If it rains on St. Swithun's day, it will rain for forty more" and the delightful "When gorse is out of bloom, kissing is out of season." Note down your—or anyone's—grandmother's

· · · · · · · · · · · ·

16　*Carmina Gadelica* is easily available and a treasury of folkloric custom. For accessible extracts, see Alexander Carmichael, *New Moon of the Seasons* (Edinburgh: Floris Books, 1992).

Traditional Remedies

Elder-flowers and berries for flu (This is actual medicine); will be haunted by the dryad if you use the wood. Wine from berries for magical use? Mother tree—always ask before using...never use wood for a cradle or to burn. "Elder tree, elder tree, give up your fruit to me..." Finish this song before autumn foraging!

* look up Bach flower associations!

Keep on with this, remembering I am a seeker after perfect, balanced health & I find my healing in nature.

Start each session: I call to the dryads for healing inspiration; I show my respect by searching this information out!

sayings: you might be surprised at how many you know. If not specifically about health, they will be attuned to the natural cycle and are all of value.

If your personal history didn't include this sort of ancestral wisdom, no problem. You are now a student of nature, so start investigating, generally and for your own geographical region. Old folklore is always fascinating and often a repository of wisdom.

From my county, Hertfordshire, here are some examples from my journal:

- Beating the bounds: walking round the parish boundary, beating stones and boundary markers with willow and birch twigs. Annual. Now done by local church. (Evidence of it from Roman, Norse, and Anglo-Saxon times.)

- Ash tree: can be sold warts! Traditional rhyme is "Ashen tree, ashen tree, pray buy these warts from me." Norse creation myth—Ash & Elm—the first two humans to be created.

- Protection (wood shavings), esp. from drowning... Yggdrasil—the tree of life!

- Split a bough and pass a sick child through it for healing. (Also passing through a natural entrance of a rooted bramble—see oak also for doorways.)

- Rowan: sacred in the ancient Finnish *Kalevala*. Every aspect holy. Twigs tied with red thread for protection—esp. Scotland? (Check this!) Necklace of berries for protection. Planted near churchyards. Associated with youth; cradles...

- Oak: "the door," the Druid tree. A portal to other realms—wood for the doors of prestigious buildings; look out for them! Always present at Druid rituals, according to the Romans.

TURNING NOW TO the energetic aspect of healing, we'll focus on qualities we might be deficient in [17] and what our trees might supply. Most of us know our chronic states of lack, but don't beat yourself up over them—they are just part of being human.

This next exercise requires movement with intent, so safety first. Relax your gaze but keep your eyes open for balance. Our muscles may respond to mental pictures or thoughts with weakness or strength infinitesimally, but if you are physically weak, nervous, or have balance issues, make sure you're near a source of support and don't be too proud to use it or do the exercise sitting in a supportive chair.

- - - - - - - - - - - - -

17 There are many that underpin our health—patience, kindness, love, open-heartedness, generosity, courage, self-belief—and, if you are currently ill, you will need strength. Choose which you need for health and achievement. Combine the exercise with physical swaying if you wish; keep experimenting and recording.

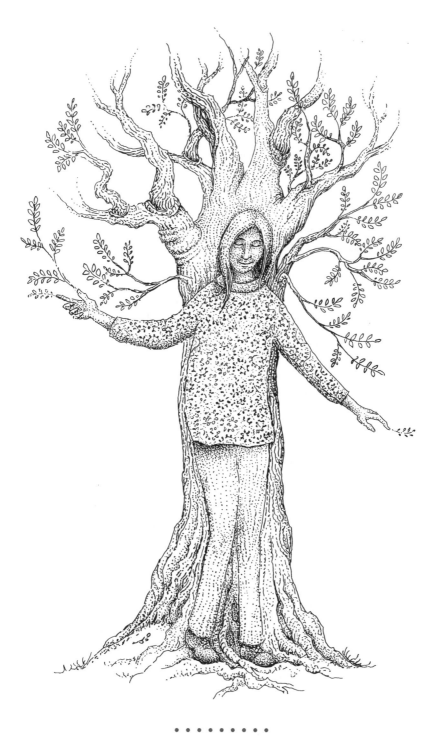

Swaying with the Tree

Envisioning the Tree Inside

Imagine your internal structure as if you were a tree. Imagine the correspondences of your trunk and its trunk; the balance of your body's arteries and veins, allowing blood flow—the vascular tree. Think of blood/sap; your and its capacity for healing when your skin/bark is injured; compare the fact that you both breathe, excrete, and can reproduce; you both move and react to your environment.

Before you go further, take time to draw this if you wish.

See your tree-self swaying, and, if it feels right, do it gently in reality as you do in your morning exercise of connection. Feel the internal flow. When you have established that, slowly breathe the name of a quality or virtue— perhaps grace, patience, trust, courage—that you feel you lack and imagine it travelling on the breeze that sways you. As your branches (arms) dip, allow yourself to feel a little unbalanced by lack, then immediately imagine an up-pouring of that quality through your roots, strengthening you. Your boughs straighten and the air supports them as the strength they're gaining flows through to their twigs and leaves. The bountiful sun shines down, filling you, and the rain washes all lack away, leaving the fresh, energised sap pouring through you. Take your time to sway with the beauty of your strength. You are balanced and whole.

Seasonal Gifts from Our Dryad

The tree's physique may indicate its gifts: the tall, far-seeing pine offers us perspective, straight-growing ash gives focus, and so on. These are constant through the year and reinforce our trust in life, belief in abundance, faith in a future that says change is inevitable, acceptance of the rightness of the natural round, and patience to allow life to unfold in its own good time.

Of the many energetic tree preparations available, the most famous are the original Bach flower essences,[18] many from trees, made by infusing in water under bright sunlight. The principle is simple, so experimenting might be the next phase of your research. You might simply quietly sit with trees to absorb these essential qualities firsthand. That's how Dr. Bach reached his conclusions, and we can devise a personalised system of unique relevance in the same way.

Magical workers know that healing always involves an interaction with "otherness," which we may access in our imaginal world. So here is a much longer visualisation, which you might like to record, leaving space for the inner images to flower. Do not fixate on literal "seeing" but on evoking the emotional response. Give yourself up to feeling and allowing impressions to arise.

18 Information readily available at http://www.bachflower.com/ (accessed April 2020).

The Healing Breath and the Elements

Luxuriate in gently moving and stretching as you relax: send your body gratitude when it responds fluently, praise it if the movements are difficult, and settle yourself into stillness. Your inner eyes show you a trail, and although it is into dense forest, the sun makes the shade inviting, and soon you're in a dimmer environment, a place of enchantment.

You breathe in greenness and energy, sensing the minute healthful particles and essences from the surrounding trees. You absorb them through your skin, your breath, deep into your body. As the trees are nourished by earth, air, fire, and water, you feel those effects in your body with every breath.

You are walking slowly, absorbing the fire of the sun to invigorate your blood and raise your vitality.

The fresh dampness acts on your watery systems, cleansing and balancing you as if a gentle waterfall flows through you, pouring all your detritus through the soles of your feet, where it sinks into the earth and becomes neutral force.

Your breath re-energises you
with every fresh breeze.

The constant earth
supports every step.

You stop by a huge tree—what sort is it? Ask permission to breathe with it. The bark texture changes, as if softening for you, and you lean against it. The tree exudes oxygen as a byproduct of photosynthesis, and you feel the fresh energy-shot as you take in this essence.

When you feel full to the brim, sink down to sit at the bole of the tree, thanking it and feeling down to the roots that hold it so stable. Rooted, connected, earthy; you feel you have been accepted by this grove in the forest; you are in the vesica piscis dimension as if the tree's dryad leans and envelops you in a hug so loving that it enlivens all your senses. You jump to your feet as its energy sends you singing and dancing down the path back to the forest entrance.

Turn and twirl, your feet moving to a simple chant of gratitude, which might start as simply as "Thanks to you, dryad of the tree; your spirit gift enlivens me," blowing kisses back at the tree with thanks until you get beyond its aura. There, turn and bow in farewell, and establish yourself as completely separate.

Feel the pull of the outside world and the need to rejoin it. Turn decisively and return to your own wonderful self, here in your body, healed and strengthened and gladdened: safe and whole and invigorated.

• • • • • • • • •

Trees are immensely giving, but we shouldn't always go to the trees with an agenda. Friends love to hang out together, after all, and the "moving meditation" of a green walk will often be all we need. We imbibe healing on all levels, just by being at one with our surroundings. The proof is how well we feel afterward.

Charm 6 Synopsis

✦ The sixth charm is fuelled by our wish for holistic healing and brings a gift from the forest: the restorative current of nature.

✦ We immerse ourselves in our local healing traditions, superstitions, and recipes, asking our dryad for help and intending healing to flow on each visit. We formulate a request to turn our attention outward and give something

back: "As I heal, so my blessings and gratitude add to the healing of the world. May my actions benefit nature."

Route Map for Charm 6

I connect to the healing of the trees; I ask what each can offer; I feel my system is as resilient as a dryad's: I drink nourishment from the earth, the sun, and the sky: I am supported with every breath.

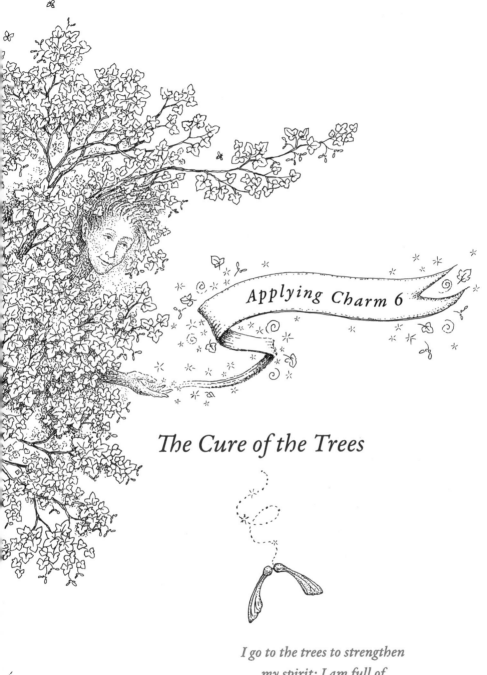

Applying Charm 6

The Cure of the Trees

*I go to the trees to strengthen
my spirit; I am full of
youthful enquiry.*

WE GO OUT to the deep green to feel its charisma and become true attractors and charmers. We are nurturing the spirit, which our dryad reminds us must take precedence. And we strengthen through respecting it—by making time to keep returning to nature and our deeper sense of self.

The healing process is complex, and there is never a morality/worthiness component to healing. Bad things happen to good people and vice versa; we accept this, and that "failure" and "success" are not appropriate words in this context. Of course, we have a natural relief and gratitude when we heal, but to castigate ourselves as "responsible" for ailments is far too simplistic.

Let's love our bodies and
give ourselves a break.

It is time to visit our inspirited trees and build on the exercises we did indoors in the last charm.

•EXERCISE•

Alleviating Old Weaknesses

Sit under a tree in reality (or imagination if you can't get there) and breathe yourself into contact with the world of nature through your body. Take a mental trip around your body and ask it where its aches and pains are. How comfortable is it? Adjust as you need to. Now take your attention away from yourself and direct it to your tree. Your image, feeling, or sense of the dryad is forming as an imaginal image deeply entwined in the actual tree. Feel that its old scars and lopped branches are part of its strength, integrated, and no longer weaknesses. Feel a kinship. You don't have to dwell on your own "life marks" from your experiences; just acknowledge that they are an integral part of you. Every experience has brought you to this place.

Gratefully let any weaknesses to be absorbed into the tree.

With each rejuvenating inbreath, fill yourself with health and beauty.

Take plenty of time with this last point before you come back to your present reality. Bring back a sense of health and strength. If you want to, stroke the part of yourself and thank if for doing so well for you. Thank your dryad in whatever way is now normal for you. Separate fully, and feel your auric field strengthened, repaired, and complete. Write your notes.

• • • • • • • • •

Healing from the dryads means expanding into their long-lived grace. We do that with our regular focus on spirit, truth, beauty, acceptance, and gratitude: all can be mediated from the cosmos through the trees.

Coming in from your walk, collect your journal and look round your living space as you did in charm 1. Note what objects, sights, or aspects you can identify in ten seconds as being nurturing to your spirit. What brings you a flash of joy? The simplest things are often the most deeply felt—a picture, the colour of a wall, the curve of a bowl we stroke in passing. Notice them all.

Then consider: Have you made tiny changes to your living space as suggested earlier? Is there now a hint of the glade, the copse, the majesty of nature anywhere? A cushion cover, green cups or coasters? It doesn't have to be big, although to suffuse your senses—even using a green light bulb for a forest ambience—can feel incredibly healing.[19] Write down all the positives you see in your journal and be grateful.

By our notice we make them more effective, so dust the bowl, wash the wall, plump the cushions. Every day we reinforce our intention to respect, nurture, and heal ourselves and our environment, so keep all these positive reminders pristine and plan to add to them. We are well through our charming process, and the main obstacle to progress is staying aware and maintaining.

Reassess the view from each window and keep looking. There is a simple guideline for allowing what you see to really sink in in a way that will make an impression: gaze for at least ten seconds to give your senses time to internalise the images. As you look out, ask what heals you. From a tower block, no colour is more healing than the blue or silver of the sky. What enlivens you? What brings magic? What gives you endurance?

Every day, gaze at these wonderful natural sights; assimilate them, and let them strengthen your spirit.

When you have jotted down the elements of your supportive surroundings—nurturing objects, changes to your living space, revitalising views—treat yourself to a restorative walk or deep meditation. What a treat!

So let's go. Affirm your intention, as usual. Use a phrase you have in your journal or extemporise: you should be getting good at this. Start your walk.

· · · · · · · · · · · · ·

19   Teresa Carey, "Can Green Light Therapy Cure Chronic Pain?" 6 April 2020, https://www.freethink.com/articles/green-light-therapy (accessed June 2020).

Ask to notice the trees as healing entities and absorb their benefits. Consciously decide what reparation you are making: of time and commitment, certainly, but maybe an extra gift to say thank you. If you are housebound, read this through and enlist others to help gather your materials beforehand. Making the gift will be an integral part of our healing meditation and can be floated out a window or taken to a tree when you are next out.

• EXERCISE •

Exchanging Gifts, Absorbing Healing

On the way to your tree, gather twigs, seeds, leaves, and grasses to bind them.

Greet your dryad in the usual way and ask for the gift of whatever you need for healing—strength, relaxed muscles, reduction of inflammation, tranquillity...

Start to arrange what you have collected into a totemic gift, which signifies the attention and love you give in return. Focus on your activity as you breathe with the dryad, asking for the healing quality that you need.

Don't become fixated on producing something "good"—if your first attempt falls apart, you can always start again. Allow your activity to draw you into a meditative space, fusing your intention with action, then let your hands fall idle.

Sink deeper into the rootedness that is your foundation of health: rest there in perfect peace for a while.

If it is the right time, feel that in imagination you can rise with the tree branches, following the extension of your dryad's tree fibres to absorb the stored sunlight of their leaves. Relax as if in a green tent of leaves, feeling as if green life is suffusing you, regenerating every cell, every system. What you did purely in imagination in the last charm, you do now imaginatively in the presence and witness of the world. Do not make an effort; expand into the feeling. Do you perceive a sense of true health as a colour, a warmth, a coolness? Where do you feel its core within you—or is it a whole-body sensation? There is no right or wrong.

Soon you will feel the need to move, to rejoin the outside world. Open your eyes and smile into the canopy of your tree. Offer the little totem that you have made to your dryad, placing it in the tree with your departing thanks. It should disintegrate very quickly, freeing the thanks and sending blessings out to the natural world.

Finish and leave in the usual way. Leaving your gift, if you do it with petition and poetry, imbues your tree with the status of a clootie tree: your gift will soon return to its natural forms. In these days of littering, an organic, discreet gift is much better than swathing trees in material!

> *"Don't change the site; let the site change you" is a wise motto.*

Healing Rhymes

Use rhymes for dryad healing—
try inventing on the hoof, but learn
some basics for

* starting my walk

* waking healing energy
  for any ailment

* using in bed for heavy
  cold

* for a health boost in the
  fall (note: make one for
  birch for the spring)

Useful phrase to adapt as necessary:

Dear [tree-name], please lead me into a
wider world of healing by your
[list three qualities]...

Maybe as you think of your dryad each night you will imagine your poppet in its branches, gradually disintegrating and taking any weakness, lack, or ailment with it. And another logical progression of your meditation would be making a healing rhyme, requesting help and thanking the dryad for it. Music, song and poetry, no matter how simple, add to your connection.

The exercise above is a whole-body experience that can easily be adapted to target your specific ailments and needs. Go back to the exercise, but after the feeling of regenerating every cell, you can keep breathing in that green, stored sunlight of the leaves. Allow it to accumulate at your heart-space, and then imaginatively direct it to any part of the body that needs it. It can subtly change colour and modify its quality as it reaches its goal: becoming red to warm, blue to cool, green to soothe, yellow to enliven and so on. This can become a go-to template for healing for every occasion.

The addition of rhymes can also add to your dryad repertoire. The following examples may help you start crafting your own.

Starting a Walk

I walk this ancient land to a meeting, to a meeting
My dryad is waiting, through the breeze I feel the greeting...

For Any Ailment

Eat an apple whilst reciting the following:

Starry heart of apple fruit
My seeds are sleeping til I plant them,
My flesh is wholesome, just like yours
Good health is every day more certain.

For a Cold

This can be used in bed for a heavy cold (magical willow = aspirin!):

Fever high I send to willow,
Every tree-breath calms and clears me
Rustling leaves my lullaby
As I sleep your magic aids me.

For a Health Boost in the Fall

> *Great maple, you joy bringer,*
> *Your flashing colours enliven*
> *Your sweet sap enriches,*
> *Please nourish my healing.*

For Connection to the Elements

You may also want to make up some movements for this. A deep breath of connection is recommended between each line.

> *Dryad of earth, I feel my rooting*
> *Dryad of air, your breezes cooling*
> *Dryad of water, cleansing and pure*
> *Dryad of fire, sun shines at my core.*

• • • • • • • • •

A major factor in our healthy outlook on life is about accepting change and uncertainty, and our dryad can help. We need to notice the lesson of the trees' seasonal changes as entirely positive. Through change, our dryad's tree is constantly renewed; and when we tune in, these changes leap out to catch our attention. Our world is made afresh with every bright dawn.

Cultivate a fascination for spotting gradual and fluid changes, and then find out why and how these changes happen, and why the differences.

🌱 One tree is in full leaf a week before its fellows nearby—why?

> *Does it catch the early morning sun*
> *first? Should you meditate there*
> *to access the healing of the sun?*

🌲 One tree is thriving—is it rooted nearer an underground water course?

> *Should you choose this for releasing*
> *old patterns and allowing the*
> *outworn to flow down and be*
> *transformed by cleansing waters?*

You are evolving a healing system. You are not inventing it but allowing it to emerge from local natural data, so it will hold coherence and validity.

Make space in your journal for month-by-month notes from your current walk. You will surely find, through the year, specific trees with gifts for all your senses: tree flowers—invisible to most, but wonderfully varied and a sign of spring; scents—of hawthorn, pine, elder, and linden, bringing joyfulness and enchantment; sights—the changing leaves of the brilliant red maple, golden yellow of elm and birch to enliven us; and taste, with the foraged fruits of walnut, hazelnut, and beech. And when the world seems inactive, huge winter silhouettes in the dark forest feed our perception of strength and endurance.

By simply noticing these, we are connecting ourselves to the dryad spirit that infuses the trees. It seems too simple, but it really works. We do not always need to find a use or a quality—we just need to admire and appreciate as the seasons turn. We need to ask constantly, "What is claiming my attention today?"

A suggestion: stop at least four times on every walk from now on to practise the ten-second trick we used earlier when looking out of our windows. Remember simply to hold fast in your memory the "pictures" you see; allow them to be absorbed into your imagination for at least ten seconds. There is a lot of competition from the everyday world, so look as closely as if you will be asked to draw what you see later.

As our internal dialogue is constant, use it! Praise the tree's physical characteristics to reinforce what you are seeing. Itemise what exemplifies the qualities you want in your life. The courage and readiness of the holly; the grace and mystery-whispering willow; the sweetness and joy of maple; the far-seeing of the Scots pine: imbibe these virtues by praising. They restore to us the balance and anticipation with which we wish to meet life.

Will the attitudes you would like to strengthen all come from your one dryad, one tree? Might your dryad introduce you to the wider community of the trees? What messages are their rustling leaves sending out?

Play with ideas and stay tuned to pick up hints from the wild.

And, if you wish to, in addition to your usual "doorway," find a special healing portal. Traditionally, this sometimes involved splitting tree boughs; we won't do that, but look for a graceful arch of boughs, a fallen branch to crawl under, or twin saplings to squeeze through. How will passing through affect your health? What intent will you set before you do so? What libation will you bring? What will be your "thank you"?

This is your life, your
experimentation, your path.
Be inventive; enjoy it!

If you are housebound, ask friends to bring you samples of trees they find on the ground. Even in spring, that time of regeneration, there is always fallen matter after a high wind. Let every sense absorb the stickiness of buds, the waves of pollen from the dangling flowers, the fragility of the scales falling from the buds as the tender leaves unfurl. At every season, reread your list and focus on what is inspirational and valuable to a healing mentality.

• • • • • • • • •

Let us now consider water as a healing medium. It can easily be seen/sensed/ felt/imagined flowing into every part of the body: it has memory and can act as a carrier, so you might try the following exercise on this next walk.

•EXERCISE•

The Energy of Water

Take a phial of water with you, with the intention to infuse the water with the healing energies of sun and tree.[20] This is an energetic exercise only—no organic matter ever touches the water.

- ❦ Sit beneath your tree and place the bottle conveniently or pour into a wide bowl.

- ❦ Set your intent: tell the cosmos, the tree, and the water your intention, and ask for their help.

- ❦ Itemise the particular gifts/qualities of the trees you are requesting if you wish to be specific.

- ❦ Ensure the sunlight through the leaves is striking the water.

- ❦ Become meditative: in your mind's eye see, feel, or imagine a current pouring from the sun and leaves. See rainbow lights and prisms and the movement of water molecules responding as the water is charged. Time is irrelevant in the meditative space; trust that what should happen will, in whatever time you have.

- ❦ At the end, state that the water is now charged for healing purposes.

• • • • • • • • • • • • •

20 There are many more detailed instructions for energising water with tree essences, but practitioners I know share a reliance on their intuitive response at the time and an understanding that close attention to the tree will show them the best way to work.

Conclude by thanking all the parties. Raise the bottle or bowl to the sun and drink with gratitude, taking time to feel the flow all around your body, and then libate the tree roots.

To replicate this at home, clean your sunny windowsill with intent and have a branch of leaves positioned so light pours through them and into a bowl of water, then follow the guidelines above.

There are as many uses for this water as you can devise. Drink a few sips to connect to your dryad.[21] Use for a specific healing meditation. Make a healing bath with your intent and add some of the water, plus any evocative scents, to conjure forest healing. Wrap yourself in a green towel afterward and go to the forest in your dreams.

Time to reciprocate for all we are gaining by using this water for the healing of the land. We don't have to specify what form this healing should take; often we won't know. Just allow yourself to think that having the right instincts will have an effect. Each time you use your water out in nature, chant or affirm that you are returning its blessings and committed to protecting nature.

---

21 Observe normal health and safety guidelines—keep water dust-free and do not keep water open for too long. If kept in plastic bottles, there will be a shelf life for the plastic.

Supporting the Land

Encircle your tree with water, blessing its strong roots and the ecosystems it supports.

Make a boundary of water drops around any area ugly with rubbish or vandalism. Resolve to do something practical about it—make the phone call, activate the right agencies for a clean-up, and start picking litter.

Send healing water into the drains to affect your cities as it flows...

Mark your path home at intervals, sacralising it with drops of water.

You can mark your path like this regularly: given the connection between water, the tides, and the moon, you might repeat it at every new and full moon or at any personally significant time—birthday, anniversary, and so on—libating the path in thanks and gratitude for your life.

Reaffirm your commitment to support the land each time you drink or sprinkle water before home meditations.

• • • • • • • • •

Before sleeping, bring to mind one of those pictures that you spent ten seconds absorbing; reaffirm your intention to support the natural world as it supports you, and sink into a healing sleep.

> *To charm, we absorb healing from the trees. Rising refreshed, we lightly, subtly, in our turn, spread healing blessings, mediated by our dryad, out to our landscape.*

Q: Why would we search for Arcadia?

A: To strengthen our dryad contact through a primal myth of "The Golden Age."

Charm 7

THE CHARM OF

ARCADIAN DREAMING

*I*n your imagination, walk along a
dusty path beneath the vast blue
sky toward a stand of pines, with hills
rising to either side and goats grazing
on their slopes. In the heat, pine resin
scents the air. Feel how this land has
been unchanged for many centuries.
The currents of earth and sky, of sun,
moon, wind, rain—all the natural
elements—are more apparent there

and mingle with your breath. You announce yourself as a pilgrim and feel a welcome.

Arrive at a tall pine. Lean against the polished plates of its bark; feel its life force, its dryad, pulling you up to the higher realms to gain a perspective on life. You seem simultaneously safely on the ground and yet elevated. You are enlivened by the unspoiled immensity of the view, where all is as it has always been. Listen to goat bells tinkling, the bees humming in the aromatic grey-green herbs, the pine boughs soughing: sense the quiet life of the earth proliferating.

Sit beneath the pine, refreshed by its scent, bathing in the sunshine dappling through the pine needles: a human alone, welcomed and held in a most ancient environment.

WE HAVE JUST visited the ancient land of Arcadia, and with this charm we touch into the spirit of unspoilt land, which is deep in our internal repository of myth.

The charm of lineage looked at specific legends; then we were invited to tell our dryads their own historic stories and share ours. Now our memories stir like fallen leaves caught by an antic breeze, and we spiral back to myth but in a simpler, deeper way. Arcadia is a country from the beginnings of story, and with the charm of Arcadia, we return to the most ancient world. We have worked hard so far and been very active in exploring, finding out, using differing media and techniques, and encouraging ourselves to expand.

This stage of the work brings an opportunity to pause and allow things to consolidate—to review what we have learnt from earlier charms and how far we've come.

Wherever we live in the world, all tree lovers can access Arcadia. It is an actual region of Greece, but it also exists as a mythic realm—a symbol for the harmonious interaction between humans and nature, inspirited and ruled by a deity that predates the Olympian pantheon. In Arcadia the essential essence of each tiny example of each species, and the overarching spirit of each species family, is expressed. It is the place of complete freedom for nature to be herself. So what is its origination?

Arcadia spills out a cornucopia of images to feed the imagination, so activate the part of you that delights in story and enjoy a lightning-swift version of the myth...

Arcas was the son of the Olympian god Zeus, who transformed himself into a likeness of the goddess Artemis to seduce the nymph Callisto, who became pregnant. His furious wife, Hera, turned her into a bear, whereupon Zeus hid the boy deep in the countryside, nursed by one of the stars of the Pleiades. Arcadia was named in the boy's honour. He became its king when his maternal grandfather offended the gods and was turned into the first werewolf.

Arcas was married and had three children with the dryad and priestess of Pan, Erato. He became a great hunter, and when Arcas was at risk of killing his mother, Callisto the bear, mother and son were both transformed by Zeus and placed amongst the stars as the constellations of the Great Bear and Little Bear.

· · · · · · · · ·

What a story—so rich in details of the inspirited land, sky, flora, and fauna, and a dryad is an integral part of it. What can we extrapolate from it?

Arcas was hidden there, making Arcadia a place of safety as well as a country of man/animal fusion into wolf and bear, of human/tree marriages and unions and of the sentient stars actively guarding its occupants. It was also the province of the god Pan, himself the son of the dryad Penelopeia—the daughter of Dryopos (Oak Face) and Hermes. Pan is famously half goat, half man; the god of wild places, of goats and their herders, companion of nymphs and satyrs. He makes magical music with his pan pipe and can inspire panic. He is the oldest of the gods and his name literally means "all-inclusive."

Having absorbed this, consider how populated this seemingly sparse Mediterranean land actually is. And yet there is space—physical, mental, emotional, spiritual—for all. Look back at the meditative charm opening you have just read on page 174. How may knowing the story of the country alter what you imagine when you return?

When we absorb the charm, which is the consciousness of Arcadia, we gain space and time inside ourselves—and this is supported by the deeper meditative exercises we can do from now on. In the first charms we have gathered a plethora of imagery. We turn the pages of memory to find bright pictures of trees in all their seasons, legends of women transforming into trees, folksongs of lovers becoming trees and uniting after death, forests sheltering the vulnerable in fairy tales. We can now relax into allowing intimations from the deepest places to arise and answer our needs at any given time. We can trust our memories, past study, our journal, and our instincts to supply all that we need.

The gift of the charm of Arcadia is that it encourages us to hold a dual understanding of environment. And there's a paradox! Earlier guidelines have made it clear that we cannot and should not try literally to inhabit Arcadia, Fairy Land, El Dorado, The Dream Time, Utopia, Avalon, the First Times, the Elysian fields or any other mythic paradise of our own culture. But when we hold Arcadia in its own imaginal realm whilst fully engaging with the real world, a dual understanding of environment and the living, essential spiritual nature that informs it, occurs. It comes when our spirit-sense—the one that connects to our dryad—is functioning, not dormant. It allows us to look with eyes ready to see enchantment.

To go deeper, to feel magical in a world as our new "setting," we must really, really understand that all the harmony, love, and support that we need is within us. Arcadia can help us internalise this radical idea.

Before we started this work, our internal landscape might be likened to a mystifying dot-to-dot picture deep inside us. Most of us have lived all our lives with a kaleidoscope of shifting, mercurial images that coalesce and then dissolve. Sometimes we have become attached to them and they have taken on a more fixed form and become our default daydreams.

Now we begin to join the dots consciously in conjunction with a primary myth of human/nature cooperation and interaction. This makes a web of communication with the help of our dryad: it is, unlike our daydreams, both relevant and helpful to our everyday lives. The more we work with this lightly and joyfully, the more our subtle structures live as a vibrant and coherent support, and the more we will feel content and truly at home in body and spirit.

You may be expert already in the arts of magic and charming, of course. If so, you will know, as all experienced students do, that revisiting territory always adds to what we already have and use.

Our inner landscape emerges from our unique life experience and under-standing. To check where you're at with this process, get your journal and be ready to answer the following question quickly, without giving yourself time to overthink.

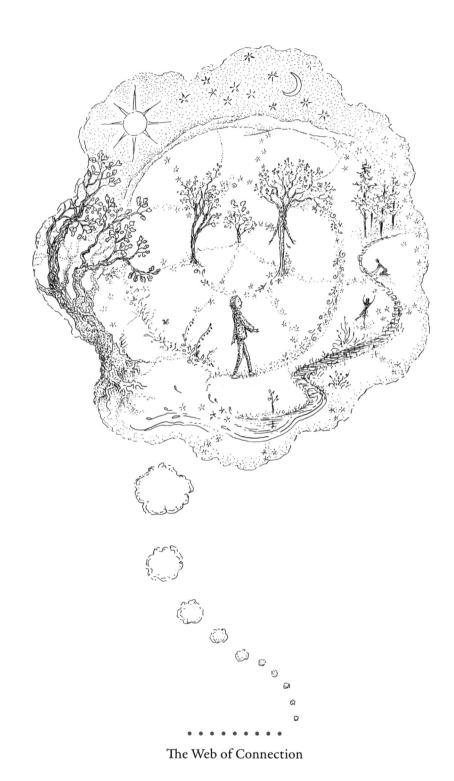

The Web of Connection

Close your eyes, breathe deeply a couple of times, and ask yourself: When you visualise or imagine your inner world, how do you feel when you emerge back into your everyday reality? Quickly write down the answer.

. . . .

....

....

....

....

Now read on...

Hopefully your answer includes many evocative words. You might have chosen *refreshed, regenerated, peaceful, calm, more able, more alive in the here and now*. Importantly, there should never be regret or a sense of anti-climax when we rejoin our outer world, which is our true home. Our inner world is to support and enrich it. But if you do return occasionally with grey feelings, retire to Arcadia and just a few minutes can help you supercharge with all you need to live your actual life to the fullest. We'll be asking our dryads for their help in experiencing this in our actual surroundings on our next walk.

The Welsh have a wonderful, rather untranslatable word: *hiraeth*. At its heart, it might be expressed as homesickness, a longing to return. I suspect that we are all born with it. Remember the expression "the yearning" in an earlier charm? That yearning is our hiraeth for the communication that brings life in abundance. Rest regularly in Arcadia, allowing new pictures and forms to arise to fit the moment. Go beyond wanting and expecting and just allow that sense of simplicity and fulness to pour in and depth to emerge. As we express this feeling, we have begun to relate differently to our everyday world.

These are sensations on the edge of mystery that are difficult to express; here poetry is a good bridge between our inner and outer worlds. Over to you! Find poems that share the sense of quiet ecstatic understanding that we read in Mary Oliver's poem in charm 3 and that convey we are a cherished part of the living world.

Checklist for Integrating Arcadia

Reaching Arcadia, or Arcady, is an important opportunity. We can rest here for a while. This charm can place several earlier themes in the context of ancient landscape.

- ○ Look back through your journal and write new notes on how travelling back to Arcady reminds us of our earlier time travelling.

- ○ How relating specifically to the pines in the landscape invites us to explore it in depth as a healing entity.

- ○ How Arcadia's feelings inspire evocative words—use these deliberately in your everyday life. Paste them on a noticeboard to keep remembering their feeling. Remember that allowing and grace are seminal qualities as we relax into simplicity.

- ○ How simplicity and meditation can bring us into right relationship.

- ○ How we are reminded to celebrate diversity as we observe the plethora of wild and mythic animals, with werewolves, she-bears, centaurs all coexisting.

- ○ Recharging in an atmosphere where spirit is more easily approachable.

- ○ Seeing the shapes and flow of the landscape and changing our perspective.

- ○ Reactivating the fascination that started our journey.

Hold all lightly as you apply your past lessons. Your dryad leads by example. The essential spirit of your tree is simply to be true to its nature and fulfil its destiny regardless of outside events. If we as humans could maintain that sense, we would be examples of living in our highest, most joyful way. "For the good are always the merry/Save by an evil chance/And the merry love the fiddle/And the merry love to dance," says the Fiddler of Dooney, whose music delights people.[22] What a relief and a wonder to be an entity to whom loving ourselves for what we are flows as naturally and unconsciously as the urge to breathe. Arcadia is the land of freedom, which allows and helps this. Travel meditatively to the inner land to connect and learn to be true to your authentic self.

· · · · · · · · · ·

We'll end with a simple meditation on Arcadia to send you to sleep. Do you now have a set form, images, or a story to help you bridge that misty space between waking and sleeping? Has your story changed since you started working to charm your dryad? Look back at the charm-opening visualization on page 174 and compare it to how you usually prepare.

Experiment, relaxing each night into exploring the magical country of Arcadia through all your stored nature memories.

· · · · · · · · · · · ·

22 W. B. Yeats, *Poems* (London: Macmillan, 1962), 30.

Nighttime in Arcadia

In imagination walk the moonlit path, sit under the trees, watch the bats, and see the dryads emerge to dance, bruising and releasing the scent of the herbage. Do not reach out for these images; allow the sights, scents, and sounds to come to you and sink deep within them. On the horizon see the centaurs and bears about their own business; lean on the supportive rocks with the guardian stars shining on you—look up, and imagine you can spot which one came down to be nursemaid to the baby Arcas so long ago...

Here are no biting insects, no bogeymen: you are in Arcadia.

> *Arcadia welcomes me in soft embrace,*
> *Allowing gentle footsteps on her grass*
> *Perfuming air, giving us space to breathe*
> *Deep, in content to watch all life roll past.*
>
> *These the gifts of Arcady,*
> *The honey, wine, and bread we share*
> *The scent of resin, kiss of sun*
> *The quiet nights caressed by air.*
>
> *This is the place of deepest sleep,*
> *Held safe by root and trunk and leaf,*
> *In the green dreaming, taste again*
> *Abundant life, simple and sweet.*

Repeat the last two lines as often as you wish...

Sweet dreams!

Use the whole rhyme above or just a single verse as you wish. It may help spark your own ideas before or after lights out. Poetry, rhymes, and chants promote our inner understanding, so ideally, when the time is right, you will write something to recite as you walk the dusty, peaceful path to the pines. Or just let a simple rhyme arise in time to your gentle walking in meditations or in the wild.

· · · · · · · · ·

Charm 7 Synopsis

❧ The seventh charm is
generated by our visits to
Arcadia and brings a gift
from the forest: a context for
our inner images, a place of
simplicity, inner certainty,
and peace.

❧ Moving gently and easily
between the realms, we
visit Arcadia regularly for
our spiritual refreshment.
We review and activate our
past lessons on allowing and

develop the feeling of a spiritual
home inside us—a landscape of space
and freedom and inspirited entities—
to people as we will.

Route Map for Charm 7

*I relax; I deepen; I simplify; I allow images of
landscape to emerge; feeling at home, I am nourished;
I thank and withdraw; I note and record.*

Applying Charm 7

Obtaining Your Passport

*Wherever I live in the
world, my love of trees is
my passport to Arcadia.*

WE ARE GOING out to meet the pastoral land of Arcadia/Arcady, taking all that the name evokes of sanctuary, harmony, and timelessness. And if mobility is limited, we will allow the essence of this mythic land to come to us, adapting the exercises creatively. To charm our dryad, we will, in some sense, become an Arcadian.

Regular communion with our dryad encourages an awareness of this land. We are continuously imbibing the lessons of slow time whenever we contact our tree spirit.

> *Gaining its gifts of a deeper sense*
> *of proportion and harmony*
> *within, so we start to express the*
> *feeling and relate differently in*
> *and to our everyday world.*

Arcadia's population includes strange, sentient beings—trees, werewolves, human bears, centaurs, nymphs, satyrs—and dryads who can intermarry with humans and have a full presence in the land. Before our rational brains protest at what it might think of as pure fantasy, let us look again at what we now know about the spirit, intelligence, and communication of the trees, attributes that in a previous age would have been regarded as supernatural.

> *Trees are inspirited; and if they*
> *are, why not the rest of the world?*

They are so extraordinary, it is important to reinforce these actual scientific findings, which have long been understood by foresters.

Have you really internalised the simple, proven facts mentioned earlier? That trees recognise family relationships and bonds and nurture each other[23]—that they communicate, and many forest workers call this "speech"? They react as warriors defending themselves and their community from attack, they can predict based on previous events, they sleep, and—attributing personality to their physical behaviour—they are gregarious or shy and may socially distance.[24]

Deep down do you rationalise these as "just" chemical reactions to external stimuli? If so, fine: but do apply that understanding also to all human actions. When our bodies are flooded with adrenalin, dopamine, glutamate, they excite reactions of embarrassment, fear, arousal; it is thought that this immediate body reaction precedes our reasoned response. Melatonin famously promotes relaxation and sleep—a chemical reacting with our intuitive response to the cycles of the earth—and yet we know that we are more than the sum of these chemical reactions, and so, we might say, are the trees.

Every year we discover that we share more than we ever knew with them. As the boughs of birch trees dip significantly in "sleep mode," so also do our muscles relax, our movement is inhibited, and our heartbeat, respiration, eye movements, and brain waves all slow. And why shouldn't many of the benefits of sleep—repairing our bodies, improving cognitive function, lowering blood pressure, aiding weight adjustment and growth in children, processing, sorting, and discarding short current events to make long-term memory—also apply to the trees, appropriate to their intelligent functioning?

• • • • • • • • •

But, back to Arcadia, and time to stroll…

• • • • • • • • • • •

23 Sharon Elizabeth Kingsland, "Facts or Fairy Tales? Peter Wohlleben and the Hidden Life of Trees," August 2018, https://esajournals .onlinelibrary.wiley.com/doi/full/10.1002/bes2.1443 (accessed June 2020) and Elisa Novick, "Tree Beings: Our Essential Companions," https://thrivingplanet.org/tree-beings-our-essential-companions (accessed June 2020).

24 Katherine J. Wu, "Some trees may 'social distance' to avoid disease," July 2020, https://www.nationalgeographic.com/science/2020/07/tree -crown-shyness-forest-canopy/ (accessed August 2020).

As we do so, we will compare our space and our dryad with Arcadia and its inhabitants. Where might they touch, embrace, connect to each other? Consider interconnection, the mysterious processes of living in a sentient world. Where does the central lozenge of the vesica piscis hold the interface of body and spirit in reality and imagination? Where might parallel worlds overlap?

As you walk, allow the rustle of the trees to whisper "Arcadia, Arcady…" or hum the words under your breath or use a rhyme or chant you constructed in the last charm. Use a wide glance to be aware of what is on the periphery of your vision. Harness your other senses; What does your intuition tell you? What catches your attention? Notice particularly birds calling or whooshing up into the sky, branches knocking against each other, the sudden flash of sunlight through the trees, or just the instinct to be attracted by a particular thing…

> *You are totally in the world and in*
> *charge, yet walking becomes a moving*
> *meditation. Set aside some time*
> *to ponder, listen, look, and hear.*

Connecting the Landscape and Arcady

Sit under your tree; contact your dryad in the usual way and hang out, just as you would with any friend.

Today we will practice writing whilst in a dreamy meditative state, so have your journal ready.

First consider the myriad of small gods and native spirits in Arcadia. Where will we find them right here? Will your dryad tell you that you've been neglecting what's amongst her roots? The shepherd's purse, the dandelions, and other small weeds—have you felt their spirit yet? All contribute their energy to the collective genius loci, the spirit of place. If you walk through a patch of stinging nettles with bare legs, you'll certainly feel their warrior energy.

Then settle down into a calmer, deeper state of awareness with the environment. Bring to mind the older times of the world and the enlarged presence of nature before mechanization and widespread invasion of our wild spaces. Invite the landscape to remember those times.

Relax, breathe, and become more meditative, then evoke Arcady within yourself and allow dreamy images to form: a landscape and all the life that it supports. Think forward now to what you would actually see if you opened your eyes. Do elements of the two imaginings overlap in any way, like a double-exposure photograph? Often they don't; don't worry.

Pose these questions in your meditative state: Which large natural features near you contribute to the genius loci? Which small entities also affect it with their presence? Bring your attention back enough into the real world to jot in your journal all the inspired flora that you notice. Be aware that there are many, many more.

Sink back down into meditation when you've done this. If it is helpful, ask your dryad to mediate and allow the answers to come through them.

Ask a question of the landscape at large: "How should I address your woodland gods and spirits and the genius loci?" Maybe the rustling of your dryad's leaves is introducing these larger entities to you? Notice each and introduce yourself in turn, just as you did originally with your dryad. Ask what each would like to say or what they would like of you. Allow answers to arise and don't rush them.

Gently and thoroughly return to your normal state of consciousness. You are separate and complete, and you thank all in the usual way. Make, find, or leave a natural gift of thanks if it seems appropriate.

• • • • • • • • •

A number of questions might arise from this meditative exercise.

Q: What if you receive a request that worries you?

A: You are an active participant, and your responsibility is to filter any request through your common sense and make sure it's safe, decent, and within your comfort zone. The trees do not take into account human boundaries: it us up to you to set them.

An example might be that you sense the genius loci would like you to visit and sprinkle water round a sacred area at night. But this might be physically unsafe in that location or you might feel that it's unsafe or uncomfortable, instincts that must be respected. You might explain and suggest an alternative; for example, that you do it discreetly in the daytime, then repeat in your own home meditation at night, to activate your work—whatever its purpose may be—remotely.

The conversation is two-way—you can and must play an active part, and always be sure you're comfortable with all you do.

Q: How can you know that you have been given
the right name for any spirit/energy of place?

A: Trust that the name that is revealed for your area, the
stand of trees, garden of shrubs, verges, and scrubland will be
the right one for you to use at the moment, even if you suspect
that you have just conjured it up from your own "la la" land.
Respectful intentions are what count; as life flows, be aware
that names may change—for who knows if a spirit only has
one name and when they will be ready to divulge one of them?
Naming is a trust exercise, so be prepared for all these variables.
It took over ten years of addressing my local stream by its given
name before I intuited the actual name I should now use.

Q: Your dryad's leaves were not rustling, which is
their usual response—what might that mean?

A: Maybe the time for wider introductions is not right on
this occasion; be patient. Or maybe your question wasn't clear
enough? Or there's a possibility that another entity might take on
the role of mediator for a particular request? In listening for your
dryad, don't ignore those rooks that suddenly start cawing and
make you twist to another direction or that movement of a small
mammal in the hedgerow. Stay open to all impressions: rigid
expectations mean missed opportunities. Maybe your dryad is
letting you know that the whole sentient world is waiting to talk—
that on this occasion we don't need a mediator or interpreter?

Amplify and illustrate your field notes when you return from your
visit or come out of your deep meditation at home. Use suggestions from
the art charm to make the notes as enlivened as the world we're exploring.
Restock your colours and draw/sketch in your margins—marginalia is a
time-honoured tradition amongst writers. Play with the "double exposure"
technique to convey and bring alive the body/spirit fusion embedded in
nature. Arcady's energetic influence can give liveliness, so hum, sing, or chant
as you work. This is precious time and space, never a chore. Enjoy!

Practice your storytelling skills when you next meet your dryad, whose species once lived in its own Arcadia, wherever in the world. Tell them of the other lands that their particular species also thrives in: everyone loves to hear about far-flung family, especially if it is distinguished by legend or myth. One of my dryads inhabits a lime tree in the UK, so I tell them how honoured their tree (the linden) is in the German culture. I tell my plane tree of their relatives who keep the air of London clean and help oxygenate the huge cities. If your dryad has no particular story, sit in the tree's shade and allow a landscape story to arise in your mind, writing it in your journal on your return.

Every hill can hold a sleeping dragon; every pool of water a nymph. Your dryad lives in a world peopled with nature spirits; imagining their stories interconnecting when we humans are out of the way helps you to make story magic!

And next, in a new initiative, bring your questing spirit to the fore once again. To get a feeling for Arcadia, we will hunt for ancient trees and woodland. This is called ancient woodland (UK), old-growth forest (US and Canada), or rain forest (South America and Australia, whose Daintree Forest has terrain that the dinosaurs would have recognised). Where is your nearest ancient pine tree, with its Arcadian associations? The oldest is said to be in California, a *Pinus longaeva*, at around five thousand years old.

As part of joining up our inside and outside selves, we connect to ancient mythic origins as we learn about the most ancient stand of trees in our area. It is doubtless being managed by humans, but that is not necessarily a bad thing. Left to itself, a hazel tree may live for eighty years, but if coppiced[25] can live for many hundreds of years. Let's take some first steps.

Realise that we naturally act differently toward ancient human beings. We are quieter, more respectful, sending out our impressions and emotions of love and goodwill to make the communication easier: and so it is with ancient trees or woodland. We are infants! Fortunately the trees nurture us, so before going to visit, word your daily petition to request a gentle response and clear messages to smooth your passage into new territory.

Checklist for Visiting Ancient Woodland

○ If you cannot get out to an ancient tree or woodland, find the nearest on a map.

○ Visiting actually or in imagination, first read up on your ancient local species.

○ Read regional natural history books to gain a local context.

○ Look for the indicators of ancientry—the flora and trees that only thrive in long-undisturbed woodland.[26]

○ Find an ancient giant tree for your screen saver. Imagine yourself hugging that tree every time you switch on your computer.

· · · · · · · · · · · · ·

25 Coppicing is managed cutting of part of a tree's growth for firewood or lumber. It stimulates growth and can prolong the tree's life to several hundred years—a rare and welcome example of how human's interactions can be positive.

26 Archangel, bluebell, wild garlic, wood anemone, primrose, and the wild service tree—More UK examples at https://www.woodlandtrust.org .uk/protecting-trees-and-woods/ancient-woodland-restoration/how-to -identify-ancient-woodland/ (accessed May 2020).

Preparing to Visit an Ancient Site or Old Tree

- ○ Tell your dryad your plans—project forward to see their green message carried by the breeze and through the roots via the wood wide web in advance of your visit.

- ○ Set your clear intent. Be happy and comfortable with it.

- ○ Plan your expedition so you will be safe and relaxed.

Visiting the Site

- ○ Approach thoughtfully and meditatively; ask for permission and wait for the answer.

- ○ Remember the portal exercise and find one that allows you in. If you are visiting a single tree, which branch invites you to slip in underneath it? Which root is providing a comfortable seat?

- ○ Feel the strong spirit of the place or tree that you already have a relationship with.

- ○ Honour it, perhaps by taking a gift of a leaf from it to this new ancient place.

- ○ Look along the edges of your sight as you stroll. Be alive to every nuance.

- ○ Notice animal movements and how they might relate to what you're doing.

- ○ Look for dancing trees, chattering squirrels, calling birds. These physical presences all carry an inspirited Arcadian resonance. All might be relevant to you.

- ○ Sketch or take pictures.

- ○ Where is the largest tree? How many people would be needed to span its girth?

◯ If you are given permission, hug it and relish the support it gives.

◯ Go safely into wilder terrain. Humans are very fragile, and you are very precious. Take a like-minded friend with you for company. When you know you are secure and ready, dream with an ancient tree, feeling its steady continuity.

• • • • • • • • • •

Our work is underpinned by respect for the spirit of the woodland. Any collection of trees houses an overarching spirit or energy, and the older and more established, the more time it has had to develop its own personality. This group soul can feel unusual and strong in a very unnerving way, and this is where your preparation comes in. This is why you ask your dryad for an introduction when you plan your trip. It is reassuring you have at least asked for an invitation and warned your host that you are coming. In a preliminary meditation, ask to be made welcome. Set your intent clearly, and ask to receive only the contact that you are able to process with joy and wonder. Take gifts for the wildlife. Show appreciation and good manners.

Then follow your usual guideline:

🍁 ask

🍁 listen to the answers

🍁 trust your intuition

🍁 keep listening

A terrain that seems welcoming at first can change its tenor at any time. And having a good relationship with a forest doesn't always mean that you are welcome to stay as long as you might wish.[27]

Listen always for the message; take the hint. Say thank you and leave. It might save you from a nasty encounter with a wild animal or your own imagination.[28] The world is not our playground, but if we heed its messages and respect them, we will have set up good relationships. Pan is lord of those wild places where dryads and nymphs are found, and just thinking of such a strong energy can evoke a frisson of Pan-ic fear in us: it's a very necessary part of our makeup if we're to be safe in this world. This short introduction is not the place to delve further into the deeper mysteries, so hold lightly, with love, kindness, and humour, and understand your own limitations. My experience has been that, though we might be tested, the higher powers will be gentle if we set parameters, come with a sincere intent, and observe, listen, and act accordingly. I act from knowing that becoming stressed is always counterproductive, so I err on the side of caution: after all, what's the hurry?

You have reached the end of your wanderings this time, so use that magical "settling down" time in the evening to review, read, draw, and contemplate the inhabitants of Arcadia and the relationship you might have to centaurs, werewolves, and myriad spirits. Had you ever thought of the dryad as a wife or mother before you heard of Erato? Think of how many thousands of seeds are born of your special tree each spring.

Consider how we colour our real world magical by such cogitations. Even in modern history in the UK, the sacred nature of trees is preserved in the

· · · · · · · · · · · ·

27 As happened to Druid friends one October, when the forest welcomed them for ceremony. Shortly after finishing, there was a strong feeling that it was then time for them to leave, which they did after tidying, leaving nothing but their thanks. It was not upsetting or worrying, just quite clear and distinct.

28 To urge caution, read "The Wild Wood" chapter from *The Wind in the Willows* and imagine yourself in the place of poor Mole.

totem trees of the Scottish clans and the traditions of the Irish[29]—opening up a whole field of personal research when the time is right. These totem animals and trees (often heraldic devices) are a significant part of the clan's culture, being praised and referenced at significant occasions. Has your family similar associations? Have any developed over the years? (Think back to early memories with personally significant trees: the one outside your childhood home, a tree that held your swing or tree house, or that tree you ran round in the park.) Are any deeper totemic connections developing as a result of your friendship with your dryad? Totems, like dryads, choose us, rather than us choosing them!

Whenever you wish, sink into the imaginal space that has been emerging: it is liminal territory, built through the previous charms, held by the long perspective back into history or far into the future. We are at the midpoint and may travel where we will. We are the ancestors whose stories will be told by our descendants.

> *To charm, we honour the ancient spirit*
> *of all trees, especially the veterans*
> *whose blessings have flowed out for*
> *generations to their surroundings.*
> *We sense their mythic vibrations*
> *back into legend and greet them in*
> *the real and the imaginal realm.*

. . . .

29 Clan and personal names that reference trees are a fascinating area of research; for example, Owen/Ewen for the yew. The Irish tradition of honouring trees was upheld by the Brehon Laws from the seventh and eighth centuries, whose punishments for damaging particular species of trees were prohibitive. Trees were classed, like humans, as nobles and commoners, with lower divisions and bushes for the less important.

Q: Why do we go beyond our dryad to embrace the cosmos?

A: To gain a feeling for the source of the regenerating power of all natural life.

Charm 8

THE CHARM OF

COSMIC CONNECTION

201

I magine you are walking to your
dryad. The approach is as ever,
though you see everything is limned
with light: a gentle, visible aura. You
are clear and free and fascinated to see
what new thing you might learn today.

As you sit at the feet of your
dryad, ask them if they will show
you something extraordinary within
the bounds of what you are ready to
receive. They remind you that you,
like a tree, link earth and sky. They

invite you to see a story of the universe in pictures and sensations. A misty veil thins to reveal a scene—a huge hill rising from water, topped by a great tree. This is the tree of life, of immortality, the cosmic tree... its great branches are thronged with every bird; every animal is perched on its branches. A wealth of green growth springs round great roots that pull nutrients from the earth and the primal waters. Its leaves feed from the air. It is supporting every life form on earth in a haze of green life force whose richness dazzles your eyes.

Then the scene fades, the mist hides it from sight, and you are aware of sitting at the foot of your tree.

Allow a few moments for the experience to settle within, then feel yourself leaving your dryad and walking back into your body, feeling fully present in the here and now.

Do OTHER LIFEFORMS understand their greatness? I think accepting the total immensity of themselves is integral to their beings, an understanding untrammelled by the rational thought that plagues us humans. Expansion into a greater life is our birthright. By taking our natural place, we are becoming expert charmers, and vice versa! All our charming exercises have worked on our understanding of liminal interactions with the sentient world. As we persist, our default mechanisms are changing: instead of needing constant reminders of our intimate connections to all, we can more easily tune into the simplicity of that truth.

So, if trees, stones, rivers, flora, and fauna are all ahead of us in taking their place in the universe, let's go to the universe and its seminal symbol, the world tree, to catch up, aided by our dryad. It is a magical truth, drawn from the hermetic philosophers, that the microcosm echoes the macrocosm: every human represents the whole; that in lesser life forms are correspondences to every part of the greater universe. It stems from the belief that the universe is of harmony and order—one of the important lessons we've learnt from our dryad. We are now acting as if this is the truth and living by it.

Similarities in Life Forms

Take five minutes to marvel that inside each of us is a seed or essence of every aspect of the cosmos. We are the mirror. Walk with it, sit with it, breathe with it; become accustomed to the idea.

Now we move on to notice similarities in natural patterns everywhere: the mackerel's skin and the "mackerel sky" cloud pattern: the waves of the sea and waving corn in the field. Gently drift over the world in your imagination for other examples—deserts, forests, under the sea—and write them in your journal. Then research to find more. Look afresh at our blood or nervous systems compared to the patterns in a tree, the veins in a leaf and the synapses in our brains and the aquatic creatures they bring to mind. Find your own comparisons in pictures of nebula, atoms, cells, the cut surface of a tree trunk...

Set your intrigue button to enjoy this. Dedicate a page of your journal to each of the three realms of earth, air, and sky. Which trees and animals inhabit liminal space? Which trees root in water? Which birds most resemble dinosaurs and reptiles?

• • • • • • • • • •

In finding connections with the living universe, we begin to focus on the most ancient and prevalent joining motif of world culture: the tree of life.

What follows is just the lightest reference to great themes; in every exploration, to paraphrase a Robert Browning poem, our reach should exceed our grasp, or what's a heaven for? In other words, we look and strive beyond the immediately achievable—and, in the case of this work, the immediately understandable. Looking as profoundly as we can attunes us to the most noble aspirations, and we do not want to work for anything less, so we turn our attention to the wide horizons of the skies.

From the beginnings of documented history, the sacred nature of the world tree has been enshrined and celebrated in image. It is a mighty tree that supports the heavens and roots deep; it joins below to above and often spans three worlds. In the earlier charms we stated, "Like the tree, I am a bridge; I connect," and so on. Each time we say it, we are referencing and joining with the prime function of both human and cosmic tree.

From Iran, Mesopotamia, Assyria, Europe, and Mesoamerica, the most ancient cultures have left us beautiful images of the tree, and it is present in some form in most established religions today. Always, no matter what or whom humankind has worshipped, the primal tree has had an honoured place in the religio-cultural view. [30]

One of the more easily accessible world tree myths is the Norse Yggdrasil, pronounced *eeg-dra-seel*. Yggdrasil is the ash tree, although there are counter claims. [31] It is especially relevant to us as its myth has perpetual flow and change, and fears for the destruction of the world by giants and gods are built into it. What should be the constants of the world—the world tree, the ocean, the balance of otherworldly realms—were perpetually at risk, and a balance had to be upheld: and that is also a very modern preoccupation.

Yggdrasil supports and connects nine worlds (some unnamed), of humans, gods, and giants—under, over, and middle worlds. And the life forms it supports interact with and affect it. A squirrel perpetually runs up and down its trunk, carrying messages—often malicious—from an eagle to the lower realms. Four harts constantly consume its highest branches, whilst deep in the lower worlds, a "wyrm"—snake—gnaws at the root beneath which flows a magical stream. Fortunately the Norns, who are the Fates personified as women, bathe the roots of the tree daily with this water to sustain it. Yggdrasil is the holiest place of the gods and called noble for maintaining its stance in the midst of these depredations.

. . . .

30 In biology the tree of life is also a blueprint to explore evolution and relationships between living creatures.

31 See Fred Hageneder, *Yew: A History* (Gloucester: F. Sutton Publishing, 2007).

The themes of our own lives are recognizable in this myth: growth and connection, constant consumption, backbiting and rumour. We have threats gnawing at and undermining the foundations of our lives and great cataclysmic forces (for the giants and gods were the great and potentially destructive forces of nature personified) endangering the planet. Here, from our past, is a myth representing our anxieties about the current state of our beleaguered world, of the cataclysmic effects of human-induced climate change. And it is a sad fact that the world (ash) tree is currently under threat from ash dieback.

When charmers reciprocate the gifts of our dryads with gifts of time and effort, we are activated by our understanding of the preciousness and fragility of nature.

This is the global scale of action we
need so that every natural token we
make and leave as a gift to our dryad
is a tiny pledge of our readiness to
help the environment in a larger way.

Research the world tree myth of your own region, country, and culture. Every religion will honour one tree as a symbol: every country or continent will have its own native species whose specific properties place it above others. Jot down what you know already of any important physical or cosmic tree before you read on.

From mythology we briefly turn to religious and spiritual philosophy, for there is also an overlap between the world tree and the mystical tree of life.[32] This grows in the centre of the paradisal garden and supplies all our needs. We will just dip a toe in those primal waters that nourish the earth from which the tree springs.

· · · · · · · · · · · ·

32 This coexists with the tree of knowledge of good and evil. Adam and Eve, having eaten of the tree of knowledge, were expelled from the garden to prevent them from gaining everlasting life by eating from the tree of life (Genesis 3:22–24).

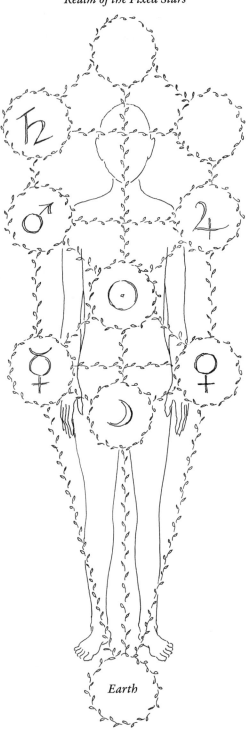

Realm of the Fixed Stars

Earth

The tree of life as commonly identified by esoteric workers refers to the diagram imported from Judaic teaching that travelled via Spain to Europe around the twelfth century. It was adopted and adapted by followers of the Western Mystery Tradition, underpinning its traditions, and is still a seminal image today. The diagram consists of ten circles (sephiroth) arranged vertically in three triangles, each embodying a quality and attached to a planet in the cosmology understood by the medieval world. Each sephiroth is connected to the others by a path, disseminating down from the heights of unknowable divinity to the realm of earth and back up again. Do not get snowed under by this complexity: the structure is revealed in the diagram opposite, so hold the idea lightly and read on to get to the main relevance for us.

The diagram looks rigid on paper but disguises its true role as a constantly changing series of interconnections encompassing every relationship in the universe. It is in constant movement and adjustment. Seeing it as three interlocking circles within which the qualities of the sephiroth interact indicates better its essential flowing, communicative nature. This approach and an original way of working with it from a Jungian perspective has been thoroughly explored by author and teacher Ian Rees.[33]

It is a specialist subject. For our purposes, we note that its middle pillar can equate to the trunk of a tree, with roots going deep into the earth. It can be applied both to us and to the cosmos—the perfect representation of the micro- and macrocosm. The centre pillar flows through us; look at the diagram to see that we stand on the earth with the Moon at our pelvis and the Sun near our heart. The two side pillars hold the planets—with their respective qualities—and are lines of communication, just as boughs and twigs all connect as part of a living entity.

· · · · · · · · · · · ·

33 Penny Billington and Ian Rees, *The Keys to the Temple* (Woodbury, MN: Llewellyn Worldwide, 2017), Kindle.

Q: What to do with all these ideas and this new subject?

A: We research if they are of interest, but there is no need
to go further. We let ideas of the cosmic/world tree as a point
of communion with our lives permeate, and see our response:
we hold this lightly. It all expands our understanding.

Q: But aren't we flying away from our objective?
How does this help us charm our dryad?

A: In every charm we are learning to be more attractive
to the whole of the world; we become so when we open to the
wonder of joining our tree spirit, our world, our universe.

· · · · · · · · · ·

We have harnessed our fascination with the minutiae of the world's wonders:
now we are reframing within this vast and infinitely mysterious universe.
When scientists disagree about the fundamental governing theories of the
universe, they leave plenty of allowable space for our most amazing imaginings to becoming a rightful, communicating part of the whole.

So, before we get out into that wonderful world, let's visit the cosmic tree
once more in visualization.

This exercise is in two parts, which I suggest you treat as two separate
visualisations. To prepare, look again at the diagram and see where the planets have a presence in the body. It might also be helpful to make a recording
if it will distract you to try to remember the whole, leaving quiet spaces for
your imaginal scenes to form, so do mark the text where you feel extra time
is needed. You are in charge, as always, and if you feel comfortable, you can
imagine travelling out into the universe. Allow time and come with respect
to this huge subject and to the process of settling down back into our present
reality afterward. Why would you rush after any deep experience? Record,
journal, and reflect. You might like to hold the thought of your dryad as a
support.

• VISUALISATION •

Connecting to the Cosmic Tree

Part One

In the way that is so familiar, breathe yourself into relaxation and let the apparent world subside. When you are ready, in your usual way, find yourself in the centre of your green space with your horizon flowing all around. Walk toward your dryad, feeling the loving contact now usual to your relationship, and express that as you wish—by stroking, patting, or hugging the trunk affectionately before you sit, cushioned by moss or grass, leaning against its solid security as if in a comfortable chair.

As you sit, you become aware of directionality: that you exist in both a horizontal and a vertical plane.

We have regularly reached up to the heights and down to the depths in our exercises, swaying and dancing. Say or sing or hum: "Like a tree, I am a bridge; I connect the earth and heavens…" and stretch and move with your dryad, activating your tall green tree-self: "Feel my roots that bond and nourish; feel my boughs that reach the sky."

Now feel also your horizontal nature; spread your arms like boughs reaching across the ground, giving you breadth and dimension. Grow, bend, and sway with this tree-feeling in the late afternoon sun: enjoy its simplicity.

And whilst you have been relaxing, the enchantment of night has been transforming your surroundings. Yet still the landscape is clear to your inner vision as you enter the green dreaming and timelessness.

When you are ready, sink back into the trunk of your dryad's tree: you are implanted, and earth energy circulates through you. Commune with the tree spirit to gain from its green strength before clearly emerging from the connection and finishing in the usual way.

Part Two

When part one feels familiar, settle down as before, and feel yourself once again in your tree-self, standing tall in the landscape, connecting earth and sky, safely rooted and grounded. When that is established, reach up. Become aware through the breeze of the energy of the upper atmosphere and out into the skies. It filters down, and if it feels right, you may let it fill you with the current of stars, the planets, the mysteriousness and hugeness of the whirling galaxies.

You have the wonderful impression that you are growing with every relaxed breath until your head and body can float amongst the stars. You are anchored by roots. They grow deep into the earth coloured by the seasons— rich green, russet red, golden, and indigo. Earth's vitality spreads through you, illuminating your imaginal body. If you are willing to be a conduit for these positive energies, let the illumination of the cosmic current meet the earth current, mingling at your solar plexus, held as a great resource in a golden chalice of light.

The junction of your tree-self's lower branches is at your pelvis. Imagine it as a silver glowing orb of moonlight, below the glow of the solar chalice that you have established, filled with nourishing light ... How does it feel to contain the moon and sun?

If you wish, your branches can hold the planets—on your right side, an orange glow of Mercury by your hip; the red of Mars by your shoulder. On your left, the green of Venus glowing at your left hip, with the deep blue of Jupiter above it.

Do not rationalise; just allow the pictures to form, dissipate, and reform as you float and explore; your earth connection is holding you safely. Be part of the universe, part of every influence and quality that finds its reflection in our everyday lives.

How do you feel this energy? As the crackling energy of potential? As love and generosity? As clarity and focus rippling in balance? Let the equal nature of emotion and intellect alternate endlessly, as they do in our lives. The current of life energy is flowing strong and true through your body, fuelled by the solidity of Earth, the rhythms and magic of the moon, the constant vitalizing power of the sun; and far beyond are the farthest planets and stars, all contributing and disseminating their influence.

You are part of an ever-present spiritual current that infuses the supportive, loving world. Just allow ... until, and soon now, your true self yearns again for its home planet, its human incarnation. Your body feels the need to reassert itself, and the scene begins to fade like morning mist.

The rustling leaves of your dryad's tree guide you home, and you move, breathe deeply, stretch, and rejoin the known world. As the last wisps of the scene fade back to its proper sphere, taking only your gratitude, you return feeling energised, loved, and complete.

· · · · · · · · ·

As always, you need plenty of time to settle yourself back into the world of action after a longer meditative exercise. Rushing to drive, keep an appointment, or pick-up responsibilities cuts short that wonderful process of slowed thought, of coming back to reflect and journal. This is part of the honouring of your imaginal life and an acknowledgement that what you are doing is of value.

Charm 8 Synopsis

❋ The eighth charm is generated
   by the influences of the cosmos
   percolating down and brings
   a gift from the forest—of
   amplifying and contextualising
   all our relationships into a
   coherent internal pattern.

❋ We follow our yearning to
   dance with the stars, bridge the
   earth, and explore the heavenly
   bodies. We petition our dryad
   to send their energy ahead and
   hold all safely.

❋ We feel the green ribbon connecting
   each of us to the anchor of our earth-
   rootedness and loving companions.

Route Map for Charm 8

I join the cosmic dance through the tree of life;
the qualities are balanced in me;
the earth, moon, and sun live in me.
I thank, I withdraw, I record.

Applying Charm 8

The Cosmic
Tree Revealed

*Working with our dryad, we
reach inward and outward
to the cosmic tree.*

OUR OBJECTIVE NOW is to continue internalizing the idea of the cosmic tree whilst—as always—enjoying a walk and communing with our dryad.

We tried maintaining an inside-outside perspective in the last outdoor section when walking completely in the actual world whilst holding the awareness of Arcadia. When we can hold awareness of an inner vision whilst making notes, we are in that vesica piscis place of flow between two states. Now we build on this, always with awareness and when we have time to visit our inner realms. So—and apologies for repeating these strictures yet again—never when driving, working, operating machinery, or seeing to the children. So much of life needs all our attention to keep everyone safe and happy that it's common sense to fully enjoy it. When we become proficient at "dual awareness," those moments of shared experience with "other" may arise without upsetting our everyday equilibrium, as precious gifts to add to our experience.

Seeing Arcadia in our world is not a one-chance exercise: if you wish, it can be an ongoing experiment and series of experiences. Used in conjunction with the image of the living tree, it will extend us to the understanding of the world in relationship to the living cosmos. Maybe this is still a far-off aspiration. But, as we're walking, exploring, and loving the million miracles of nature as we go, there is no way that this and every other walk will not benefit us. So...

So out into nature: and a challenge. Before you read any more, or any of the ideas below, ask yourself: How will you activate the feeling of the tree of life within and without as you approach your tree, chat with your dryad, and stroll?

Write four or five ideas in your journal now, then go for a walk and put them into action. You have written your own guidelines, so enjoy your walk and write it up in your journal on your return.

I hope that that was liberating and enjoyable; I'd love to know what you wrote. There are suggestions below for your next walk. Are they more or less effective than those you're using? Remember there is no right or wrong, just what works for each of us.

Checklist for Connecting Vertically Before Walking

Before setting out, practice your "tree swaying":

- ◯ Open to your tree-self and send greetings out to your dryad...

- ◯ Allow the welcome of the world to encourage you...

- ◯ Then extend—your roots going down not only into the earth but to its central generative power...

- ◯ And extend up to the far reaches of the universe and all that fuels its great movement.

You can do it all in a flash! Like a shot of caffeine, feel the connection through you, then let it go whilst its benefits remain. It's time to go walking.

If you feel you've skimped on the earlier practical charms, don't tell yourself off—we're all human and do as well as we can. Take a break to review and practice little and often until you can metaphorically jump into an expanded state with ease.

Q: How do we know when we're adept at this?

A: When we can evoke the feeling we wish quickly and clearly, control how long we stay in this state, and, most importantly, return fully when we finish. The trees will wait for as long as it takes.

• EXERCISE •

Sensing the Tree's Aura and Absorbing Green Resilience

As you approach your tree, focus beyond it with relaxed eyes. You have done this often, and all that practice is paying dividends.

Gaze gently, focussing on the sky beyond and behind your tree. Very soon the aura of your tree shimmers subtly and shows its reaching movement up to the cosmos and out across the earth to your inner senses, if not your physical eyes. Allow a wave of love to course through you and salute its spirit. See or perceive or imagine or sense the shape of the dryad as it becomes more present to meeting you, and sit with it with the usual greetings. Settle down.

Breathe with your dryad. Your awareness of your "personality self" recedes until you feel just another part of the living landscape. Practice your soft focusing to show you the auras above the grass and round shrubs and moving with the swiftly flying birds. In your inside-outside awareness, ask yourself what colours these shimmering outlines might be.

🍁 Do you sense an almost invisible glimmer or a rainbow of colours?

🍁 How does each tree's aura connect to another, and how do the trees' movements combine auras in a great whole? Are these connections one visual representation of the genius loci?

Wander away from your dryad's tree now.

Find a discreet vantage point from where you can study it. One of the neighbouring trees will give you shelter and a back rest if you ask politely. Then relax.

Firstly, just really notice, as if for the first time, the physical reality of your tree. It's been some time since we took in the physical proportions, colour, stance, and anchoring of our tree.

When that is imprinted on your mind, close your eyes. As you hold your tree in your mind's eye, allow the tree within you to emerge, and feel its characteristics in the same way.

Open your eyes. Study the tree's movement.

And close, sensing the movement of your trunk, branches, and twigs.

Open your eyes: gaze beyond to the sky and see/sense the energy field around it.

And close, seeing the aura of your inner tree reaching out.

Open to see the tree's aura responding.

Imagine the tree is showering light energy down and you have light tendrils extending up. In a middle meeting ground, there is a chalice filling from which you can imbibe tree qualities: pliancy, lissomness, suppleness. There is no sudden or violent change, just a subtle influence. If we accept it, this can start to erode the rigidity we have all worn as armour for many years and replace it with an adapting, limber attitude of grace. Do not rationalise; just allow.

Be profoundly aware of green
strength, green life, green resilience.

The resources of the universe are all encapsulated in this tree energy.

And allow the feeling to recede, stored safely within. Let the sounds of the natural world lead you back into your body, and make your usual check of being completely back, happy, whole, and yourself. In the usual way, stand, stamp, feel your body, and love being in it.

• • • • • • • • •

It's important to keep noticing signs from the interactive world. The first time I started this exercise, a car horn got stuck, a man started shouting, and two walkers appeared out of nowhere. Needless to say, I didn't continue. Shortly afterward, I found the perfect spot and continued uninterrupted.

As we are still in the realm of ancient times, you will probably want to revisit those old, huge trees you identified in the last charm to resume the conversation. Take some seeds for the wildlife or a leaf from your familiar tree. If they are too far away, use your photographs to remind you of their antiquity or have the exchange below with them or with your own dryad if that feels right or is more practicable.

Ask those ancient trees: How does your tree mirror the great cosmic tree, the tree of life?

Your answers do not come in sentences but in noticing. As you wait calmly, you realise that being under any tree can activate your tree-self. Maybe being a tree in the world of form gives each an automatic connection to the essence of "treeness" that is the tree of life in the more subtle realms?

Remind yourself that there is a micro-atmosphere under every tree; your tree supports many life forms—flora, fauna, insects, lichens—mirroring the great tree that supports all life. Look for these tiny forms that colonise near and on the tree: itemise them, record them. When you get home, research those invisible to the eye.

> *The wood wide web of roots and*
> *fungi beneath you connects across*
> *entire countries and continents.*
> *Listen for the dryad's thoughts. Sit*
> *with the tree; trust the process.*

If internalising the idea of the cosmic tree resonates with you, keep relating back to it. If not, regard it as a fascinating tangent for the moment.

Who knows when this background knowledge will become relevant? To continue, choose the time when your imaginal self is most active and go back to the exercises to strengthen your tree, earth, water, star, moon, or cloud gazing/connection. If you haven't yet found your optimal time, experiment.

At some stage, the world will reassert itself and your studies might seem to demand too much energy. That's fine; this process is organic, not mechanical. Just keep in mind the fascination—a guideline for a magical life—and allow yourself some fallow time.

If you feel you need a fresh impetus, then, as if tending a smouldering fire, rekindle it with fresh, bright twigs. Go back and remember the ideas that flame into life within you: reread the charms and your journal to find them.

There is much slow building in dryad charming, but every exercise must be approached as if it is fresh and new—and it can be a real challenge. If you keep seeing the same things, having the same responses, you might have slipped back into a habitual sleepwalking mode for getting through life. Is the pull of the world—so insidious and all-pervading—influencing you away from the magic of your studies? Do you need a rest? Reclaim your birthright in nature: reawaken through your senses to what is actually around you to see that it changes every minute.

And then, health permitting, let's find a new, higher landscape.

Q: Which trees and landscapes would remind
us of the cosmic tree or the tree of life?

A: Trees that sustain; trees that nourish; huge trees.
Large views that show us more of the world and sky.

Firstly, landscapes. Every hill is a liminal space, a meeting of earth and heaven. With a larger view of the world, we truly feel that we are the bridge between sky and land, anchored but able to float free. It is wonderful how physical space leads to a feeling of space internally, and this can make a hill a place of epiphany—of insight and revelation.

We are primed for an experience by the preparation we have to make: physical exertion, walking into a more rarefied atmosphere, a slight change of temperature, an expanded viewpoint, reassessment and rest when we reach our goal. Freedom from the cares of our everyday life. You may have to designate a special time and go to a special place, but don't let that put you off. But if time is tight, then after the hill work, you'll find simpler ideas to follow immediately.

So, go to a hill, having sent your greetings and introduction before you. Hum a climbing chant as you walk to introduce yourself and praise the plants beneath your feet. Use all of your senses as you climb. Are there trees growing on its slopes? Notice them; send greetings from and to your dryad. In a walking meditative state, you are full of ongoing communication within a great field of calmness.

Then circle the top, absorbing all the view. Stretch with the wind and sky; step and bounce on the earth.

If it feels right, lie down and feel rooted and secured. Gaze at the sky and imagine the spinning of the globe carrying you safely. This is the ideal place to proceed to a longer imaginal exercise if you are uninterrupted and in a safe space.

Make the space your own, and that includes making use of all your disguises—a book on your lap, a thermos—to make you fit in with any other walkers who might arrive. You are just a hiker taking your ease, resting in the sun ...

The View from the Hill

Think down to the roots of the hill that you are sitting on and to the underground streams that irrigate the land. Then drift in imagination to a seed emerging from the first hill rising from primeval waters. As you watch that seed, it is as if your body is responding to its movement, its growth.

It puts out its first tender shoots—there is an uncurling in your body; it reaches up to the sun—and, with it, you gradually stretch and rise. See the first tree grown: you replicate this every time you are upright and open to the natural elements, in full leaf, a mature tree.

By the magic of the first creative impulses of the universe, the tree is a home to every living thing in the world, and your outstretched arms, great boughs of the tree, effortlessly hold all the birds, animals, insects, microbes, fungi, algae, and lichen of your region.

You are a pool of dynamic stillness. Around you the higher life forms ceaselessly move and call, light as gossamer, flowing from you and out into the world to people it. A shade of a wolf leaps from your branches; an eagle soars above your crown. Myriad lifeforms flow in a shadowy procession, taking their place in the world, filling the air with joyous animal cries and birdsong. Watch the endless movement as muscle, bone, and sinew grow denser; the first animals run to find their places in the world.

Briefly having an understanding of the tree of life, you empathise with its capacity to endlessly generate and support. And you are supported and nourished in turn, held by the earth and air, effortlessly, as the scene settles to what it is in the outer world and the light pressing your eyelids and wind on your cheek call you back.

Allow the scene to fade. As you return to the populated world in all its diversity, notice particularly the impressions as you open your eyes when you are still in a liminal state. Gaze out, feeling your capacity and capabilities, your responsibility to succour and nurture. Press your hands to the earth and affirm that you are fully back, fully present.

Drink your coffee; make your notes. Bless your experience!

. . . .

And, as we simply walk for the pleasure of it, there are many simple and easy ways to connect to the eternal tree, and deeper considerations.

Internalise the idea of being nourished anytime you walk through an orchard or by a fruit or nut tree. Actually eating fruit from a tree as we walk—after asking the dryad—can be part of a moving meditation that literally joins inner and outer experience. All orchards are magical, timeless spaces, in my experience.

In a reflection of the cosmic tree, all trees are succouring. Go out with that in mind to find those that house the greatest number of species.

Myths of the first tree usually place it near or over water: find a tree by water in your region. Devise a meditation on the waters of life and the trees that arise from them.

Practice being the tree that joins in your walks and meditations, and play with ideas of how that applies to and affects your everyday relationships.

Be kind! Before you kill that spider, that mouse, that bug, or allow your child to stamp on that snail, identify with your tree-self. Does doing that affect your actions? Should it? Sometimes yes, sometimes no. Either way, you will have worked out the reasons why you act as you do.

Allow the eternal nature of the universe to become part of your thought. Make your doodles cosmic. Can you see a connection and influence between cosmic aeons of time, the life of a tree, and our short lives? Does considering the orbital nature of the universe give you a feeling of the spiraling nature of time?

This last is especially for the natural philosophers amongst us. Expanded viewpoints, perspectives, and thought all help attune us to the mindset of our long-lived dryads.

These study sessions seem to be ending now with suggestions for bed-time—the ideal liminal time to range through the imagination, consolidate our new ideas, and allow them to settle during sleep. This time, wander again along the Arcadian path toward the pine that joins the worlds.

Describe the scene to yourself as you climb the hill; allow the sky to darken as you get higher, and feel the levity of the moon lifting you effort-lessly into a stellar world of wonder. An echo of the shining moon glimmers in your pelvis, the sun is reflected at your heart, and around you orbit the major planets, which pour their energies as rainbow lights through the dark-ness, through the cosmos. Drift into sleep, and sweet dreams.

> *To charm, we honour the primal,*
> *vigorous, diverse urge of nature. We*
> *share a spark of the life force that*
> *fuelled our world so many aeons ago.*
> *May we feel the essence of eternal*
> *tree-ness, eternal human-ness, and*
> *our mysterious moon, sun, and*
> *stardust beginnings deep within.*

225

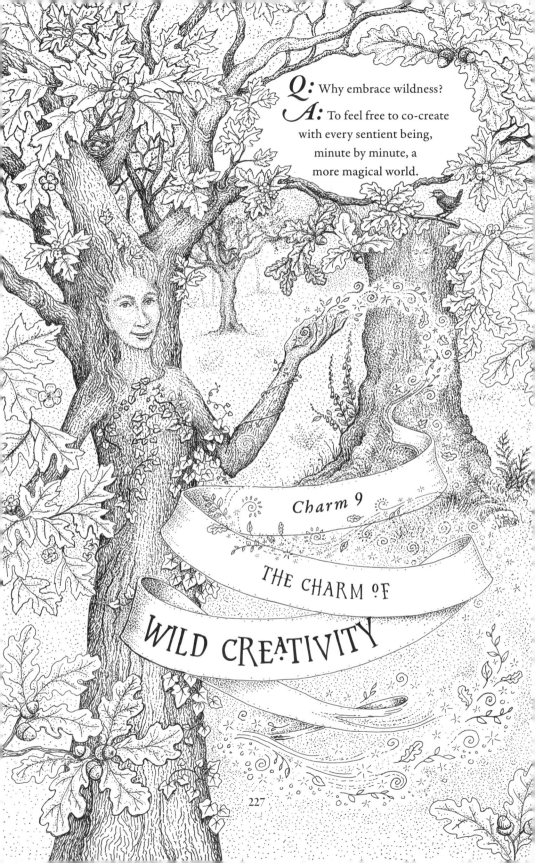

Q: Why embrace wildness?
A: To feel free to co-create with every sentient being, minute by minute, a more magical world.

Charm 9

THE CHARM OF

WILD CREATIVITY

*B*reathe, and your inner tree sense awakens: your unique, perfect tree-self. A life-giving elixir—blood or sap—flows through you, re-creating you with every oxygenating breath, and you are constantly discarding, making way for new growth.

Drift through the seasons, acclimatising, propelled by your breathing, totally at home. Notice that your

trunk has a smooth-edged hollow at your heart space, a mysterious place of meeting and balance. Now view the tree-self you have just felt. The hollow is potent and magnetic, drawing your eyes; how have you only just noticed it? From it, two large eyes look out—it is an owl, seeing all; silent, discreet, wise. If it feels right, it can become the symbol of your spiritual and creative impetus. It holds awareness: it is alert but still. Be as a sleeping tree as you rest in this space for a few moments and allow its potent stillness to replenish you.

You are being called back to the everyday world now. Allow the images to fade, returning fully to your revitalised body to stretch, feel your separateness, and journal.

THIS CHARM SETS us on uncharted waters into wild creativity. And this lack of boundaries is usually accompanied by frustration: not being sure how to start is our challenge.

We've been dipping our toes into this pool all along; let's continue gently. Through our experiences we've developed a much freer way of thinking and interacting. The potency of the earlier charms has been activated by internalizing, and we are feeling the effects.

The thrust of the work has been to look at the world afresh, to reframe our relationships, and now we can combine all that to carry our free, expansive understanding forward into the rest of our lives.

In this charm we help to consolidate it all with the use of the breath.

We are joining our inner and outer worlds—of spirit and of matter; of our socialised and our natural selves; of ourselves and wild nature. Breathing in and out is an actual physical enactment of this inner and outer exchange, a symbolic act, and we do it every minute of our lives.

• EXERCISE •

Being Breathed

I have given no firm instructions for breathing exercises for three reasons. Firstly, I'm no expert to advise you; secondly, following rigid instructions can produce tension and anxiety; and lastly, many of you will already have a preferred method.

So we each need to find a comfortable rhythm.

The suggestion below will start us all in the same way with the simplest of breathing exercises, but it is only a guideline for those who would appreciate one. So, if you wish and it feels comfortable—

* We count the breath as we breathe into the diaphragm through the nose ...

* We notice the quiet in- and egress of the breath through the nostrils and the lungs inflating and deflating ...

* And we count it back out again.

It can be helpful to count the outbreath backward, so: in 1, 2, 3, 4 and out 4, 3, 2, 1.

Many people feel comfortable with a 4/4 rhythm, or 4/8, whose slower outbreath can relax and calm. Experiment and trust what is right for you. The important elements are the measured breath—no racing or snatching— and diaphragm breathing, so the lower area of the lungs is inflated and the shoulders do not rise.

Settle into that natural rhythm, yet breathe with awareness. And soon, with the right visualising—whether connecting to your own dryad or the tree of life—you may feel as if you are breathing in sync with the universe or that the universe is breathing you. Play with this idea; what effect does it have upon you?

We need oxygen (O) to live. We breathe out carbon dioxide (CO_2). Our dryads' trees, using the energy of the sun to feed the tree through photosynthesis, use the CO_2 and produce oxygen. So far, so wonderful.

Even more amazing, every breath is also a connection to the most ancient—pre-dinosaur!—aeons of earth-time, and this is how: a tiny (1 percent) but key constituent of the air we breathe—argon—is a constant: it is inert, meaning that it is never changed by this process, so the argon component of the air we breathe has literally been breathed by every generation before us, including the dinosaurs. What implications!

Through argon, we are sharing breath with every human and pre-human role model we can imagine from times past, with all sentient life and the earliest trees before the dawn of humanity.

Therefore, we are breathing, in part, the breath of our hero/ines: of ancestor trees so old that they are now being burnt as coal. Argon, because it is never changed by what is around it, is used in scientific experiments for shielding, so it has the qualities of being protective and defensive, with a steadying implication of continuity in our times of frenetic change. As we take each breath, be aware of sharing not only with this known world and everyone in it, but an older world, long gone and forever unknown, which has informed ours.

We are breathing in mystery.

So a simple breathing exercise lets us breathe and be breathed by the whole cosmic order, as symbolised by the tree spirits, the dryads. And we can extend that further: Rudolf Steiner[34] said that the earth itself has a daily

. . . .

34 Early twentieth-century Austrian philosopher, scientist, and founder of anthroposophy, a system with educational, agricultural, therapeutic, and artistic methods to improve health and well-being through nature.

and annual breathing pattern, and that has now been substantiated by science.[35] Having experienced the sentience of the dryad, we now apply that understanding to the entire globe. There is a particular connection between earth's energy and ours at dusk and dawn, so the early hours or the end of the day might be an optimal time for working. Even if it's for five minutes in bed before we fall back to sleep, it is all worthwhile. Argon can remind us of our interrelationships.

Being under a tree can activate our tree-self, and we have discovered real benefits through being present and aware. Now consider that the strength of the trees comes from an effortless connection to a regenerating current. Imagine that this current is an essence of "treeness" existing in the subtler realms that influences our world of matter. Now, to set the seed to continue the work when this book is a memory, can we connect to the idea of a realm of creative force informing our world of form? If so, as humanity is our state, is there also an essence, a perfection of "humanness," in the more subtle realms? Maybe what we are gaining from the trees is trust, and maybe trust comes from relaxing into expressing an aspect of the perfect model. Perhaps a willingness to accept this hypothesis will help open a conduit to that regenerating place?

This charm awakens fully an essential element of our humanity that we've been murmuring to as it has slumbered: the need to be creative. The difference between living a life and existing, just coping, is a vital distinction, and we all want to live. We need to embrace a creative outlook as if it will save our lives, as—in the most important sense, that of nurturing the spirit—it will. We're embracing being a flawed, wonderful life form, and our strengths and weaknesses are our tools. The dryads have helped us know ourselves without judgment, so we use that to develop the unique gift we will offer to the evolutionary tide of life as it flows.

· · · · · · · · · · · · ·

35 Curt Stager, "The Surprising Ways Your Breath Connects You to the Entire Planet," *Wired* (17 December 2014), https://www.wired .com/2014/12/your-atomic-self-how-your-breath-connects-you-to -universe/ (accessed August 2020).

Do not fret about what your unique gift is. Just look outward to see how to do what you love. What is happening in your world, and what do you bring to it? What time can you free up to allocate to your creative impulse for gardening, painting, cooking?

Q: How are we defining creativity?

A: In this context, it is doing something you love in order to bring into the world something that was only an idea before. Perhaps an idea in the ether is waiting just for you to notice and harness it.

Q: But how can creative cooking possibly help the evolutionary tide?

A: Every happy, fulfilled human is in the flow: being that person is adding to the good in the world—a valuable balance to all the unfulfilled people. And being in the flow also inclines us naturally to applying our gifts as and when needed. So take the first step and trust to the rest.

· · · · · · · · · ·

Imagine doing what you love every day: what a thought! Imagine joyfully transforming the idea of "boring stuff" into "the stuff that supports the life I love." These are wild, freeing thoughts to work with.

At the top end, our creativity might take a complex form that benefits nature—masterminding an ecological campaign, for example; but it needn't. That's not the point. Forget the ingrained conditioning about selfishness; we must focus on ourselves to find something simple that makes our hearts sing. That's the criteria—if you generate an idea that doesn't fill you with energy, ditch it and allow the next to arise. Making time to earth our creativity in an activity with a concrete result recharges us. It is fuelled by a focused and charismatic impulse as we lose our self-importance and self-involvement.

How to get the kids to school:
move nearer...daily taxi...buy Chitty
Chitty Bang Bang...charter an
aeroplane...move them to a nearer school...
car share...home school...make them walk
it to build resilience...enrol them at the
school breakfast club...adjust our work
patterns to free up time/car...buy them
bicycles...petition for a school bus...private
hire...board them out during the week...
camp in the adjoining woods...*cycling
buddy system with those living nearby,
with rota for parent supervision...ask the
kids for ideas...meet other parents in the
same situation

And, for space to ponder, commune, and let ideas arise from the depths, we go to nature, to our dryad—who also permits us to be wild!

To think out of the box, ditch binary yes/no, right/wrong thought for the "three options," which opens up possibilities. Find a tree whose leaves have multiple leaflets—California buckeye, horse chestnut, honey locust, ash, acacia, and so on: draw one in your journal now. Press such a leaf and keep on the nature table as an *aide memoire*. Before you need to use this image to help with an important decision, have a practice. Think of a small, less than perfect thing in your life—just for five minutes, so nothing too emotionally charged: a situation that is sort of okay but could be bettered. Draw a leaf with leaflets, and fill each in with a different perspective on your situation. You can forget "sensible" in favour of lateral thinking until each leaflet has a different idea, viewpoint, or suggestion. Reviewing simple aspects and fashions of our everyday lives and thinking outside the box regularly—Why cereal only for breakfast? Why not drink from the saucer? Why not button clothes on the other side?—introduces us into freshness, and it could help prime our receptiveness to nature and our dryad's wood-wisdom.

Problem Solving with Dryads

As an example, see our dryad diary for brainstorming ideas on how to get the kids to school. The first part of this entry was as follows:

> Dreamed all this sitting under a horse chestnut. Breathed with it, thought of its flower "candles" illuminating the problem, set my intent, chanted some rhymes to get rid of the stress, felt the balance between myself and dryad relaxed, picked up pen ... Started by drawing a horse chestnut leaf and wrote suggestion in each leaflet—filled 4 pages with leaves! Notes re: timings & work commitments (write everything, no matter how ridiculous)

> *Actions:*

> This afternoon: carry this list back to the trees & have another think in situ. Will anything new arise?

> * Discuss starred suggestions tonight after work with whole family.

> Ring nearby parents with a possible plan.

Work on your creativity, the magical element to living; it is the bringer of enchantment, the expander of our imaginations. There are more suggestions in the next (last) study section.

Now, how do we embed our theme of developing new relationships into our modern world of the everyday? If we can just bring the context of the dryads and sentient life into daily life wherever we are, we have set ourselves on the course of a truly magical life, regardless of circumstances. That may be well underway, and our focus on creativity will consolidate it. So let's have some fun with those arts seen as too mundane or lightweight for a quest! They're valuable, having formed before we're even aware of it. For where are our roots? They are, mundanely: in the actual earth, in our family and the family/relationships we have subsequently made, and in the culture in which we've grown.

So is there, in the easily disposable coin of pop culture, a resonance of our human/cosmic relationship?

Q: But surely pop culture just skates on the
surface and can't have a deep effect?

A: Not so: pop music is pervasive, inescapable, and has
a huge influence. What were your earliest influences? TV,
CD, radio, cassette tapes, or another antiquated system?

. . . .

Pop from the 1960s is still influential, fuelled by protest and the desire to live counter to the dominant culture. It was a time both of innocence and great energy; it is relevant as, spiritually and creatively, we also are trying to revision the world. So it's worth saying that one change from those times is that recreational drugs are now widely agreed to be counterproductive to a spiritual path.[36] But the wish to escape the trammels of rational thought and become the best and most fulfilled we can be remains valid.

. . . .

36 No disrespect to any paths for which drug use is a traditional part of
   spiritual development, but as the spiritual disciplines that safely hold
   and support their use are not integrated into our Western culture, in
   general, drug use is best left alone. The particular path we're exploring
   has no known history of support, parameters, or use.

Imaginations were fired by the space programme of the '60s, and they found a new expression in the cosmic themes, as in "Space Oddity," "Space Truckin'," "Space Cowboy," and the chorus of the classic "Woodstock" by Joni Mitchell reminds us that the elements of our own bodies were made in a star and many have come through several supernovas. How amazing! We come from the cosmos, we are carbon based, and we share that with every living thing on earth: a connection, in a multiplicity of diverse expressions, prompting our deeper selves; lyrics can remind us of this.

Love, that ennobling emotion, is also served well by expansive cosmic imagery. Separated by three or four decades, from Sinatra's "Fly Me to the Moon" to Coldplay's "A Sky Full of Stars," there are a thousand examples. Our memories and radio/random streaming are crammed with comparisons between love, the beloved, or life itself and the starry realms.

From an earlier charm, remember: if we truly love life and embrace it as the bridegroom, we will feel the overwhelming urge to join with the universe. To instantly experience the love of living, sing and dance along to any version of Nina Simone's "Feeling Good," whose lyrics include all sentient life as integral to the feeling: it's ecstatic! Its message of peace and freedom for all gives it gravitas, so if you listen to one song in this charm, make it this one.

Classical music is also readily available so readers of all tastes can access this route—*The Planets* suite by Holst, "Also Sprach Zarathustra" by Richard Strauss, Beethoven's well-used "Moonlight Sonata," or any one of a thousand film scores.

One cannot be permanently dancing round one's kitchen, but it can happen a lot, easily. Probably it should happen more than it does! So, have you kept on dancing and singing from the suggestion in an earlier charm? And if not, ask yourself why they didn't become habits. It's very easy to jump back into our comfort zone when we've done the experiment, but please, in the spirit of wild creativity, of pushing the boundaries, find a cosmic tune to dance to, from a chair if mobility is difficult. This is a serious invitation to try a series of spontaneous exercises over the next week, so jot it in your journal now as something to achieve.

Taking a magical feeling into the world, become tuned into atmosphere, wherever you are. Seemingly mundane places and situations can carry a mythic signature, a reminder of our own country's Arcadia. If it feels right, go—not to the trees this time, but to the haunts of humans, the places where we work, shop, and do our business—to re-enchant our world.

Connect to your inner tree-self and your dryad, then wander round, seeing your surroundings with fresh eyes.

I will carry forever a glowing, golden-leaved tree seen suddenly afresh in a heart-stopping split-second in a small city. It was a transcendent moment that brought tears to my eyes, and I had to find a bench immediately to sit and absorb it. There is so much of the natural world in the urban environment: the tenacious weeds rooted in the paving cracks, the vast stands of loose-seeded plants; the ranks of nettles springing up in defiance of humanity's concrete. Breathe with the huge oxygen-giving marker trees, thanking them. What nymphs dance near the fountain in the mall? What grail knights walk the sidewalks? What busker's music can conjure in a phrase another place and time? It is the artists'—our—job to reimagine, to see with fresh eyes.

One poet, Edmund Clarence Stedman, had such a moment in the economic heart of the USA:

> Just where the Treasury's marble front
> Looks over Wall Street's mingled nations...
> Even there I heard a strange, wild strain
> Sound high above the modern clamor,
> Above the cries of greed and gain,
> The curbstone war, the auction's hammer...
> And as it stilled the multitude,
> And yet more joyous rose, and shriller,
> I saw the minstrel, where he stood
> At ease against a Doric pillar:
> 'Twas Pan himself had wandered here
> A-strolling through this sordid city...

The demigod had crossed the seas ... to these

Far shores and twenty centuries later. [37]

Pan has wandered from his haunts in Arcadia to New York to enchant it. His music transforms each working person into a cyclops, a dryad, a faun— full of infectious gaiety. The message is that nature throbs in our veins, and when we are exposed to it, we are enlarged, so we must work with that influence instead of suppressing it. It can be accessed with every gust of wind down a city street.

Occasionally, the impetus of a particular historical age will use mystical nature particularly as a major theme. It is usually in a context of increased industrialization, a dependence on rationalism, and political upheaval[38]—a state of the world that sounds familiar to us all. The exciting, relevant, and reassuring message from this is that there is a European tradition of the healing power of creativity in troubled times. And we can be part of that personal healing, at the very least.

The arts have been seen to transcend the present ills of individual and society and reimagine a better way of living our lives. One of the larger intentions underpinning this book has been to learn this, through studying the charms. The thought that our artistry and inventiveness can reimagine the world inspires us to embrace our creativity; we might even ask what better use is there of any life?

To prepare for this, let's go within to sense the possibilities of enchanting our urban landscape.

. . . .

37 Edmund Clarence Stedman (1833–1908), "Pan in Wall Street" (1867; public domain).
38 For example, the English Romantic poets living circa 1750s–1850s— Blake, Coleridge, Byron, Shelley, and Keats.

Enchanting the Urban Landscape

You are breathing your way into your inner place to walk, in imagination, around city streets under a cloudy sky in the drizzle.

There are few people on the streets; it is warm, and you are comfortable in an internal world allowing you see the usual with fresh eyes.

Stroll and start to see the rhythm of the buildings and roads, the sweeping curves of the roads, the elegance of the roundabouts, each planted with trees whose auras move with a green shimmering as they sway. Copy their shapes with your arms as you walk; no one will notice you attuning to the pattern and flow of the city. The traffic lights shine like jewels in the distance. There are few passersby, whom you feel are in the same wavelength. Their eyes are like dark pearls as they also witness a magical scene. The skyline is jagged, evidence of its history. The roofs are shining in the rain with myriad gleams; the tiles are deep aubergine, slate grey, ceramic russet—a glorious palette of colour. Stretch your arms high, sweeping an imaginary paintbrush as if you could re-create them on canvas. The puddles have rainbow lights in them and splash with diamonds as the rain falls. It drips from a leaking gutter onto your head and down your neck: you shiver and feel baptised and accepted into this human environment.

Listen with fresh ears to the constant tune of the water trickling into the drains and the leaves rustling to a different meter with every breeze through the tree-lined street. The deep pulse of life is made up of a million infinitesimal sounds, with nature as the great conductor. A dog barks; a car toots; you hum with the song of the city, the orchestra of tyres and calls and bird and leaf never repeating a phrase in the concerto.

Activate your sense of smell as you pass a mound of wet leaves; a faint whiff of fumes through the clean dampness makes your nose wrinkle. Imagine a city powered by clean energy. It is lost in the smell of baking and coffee from a patisserie now—all are part of your world. Your sense of feeling leads you to dig your fingers into the crevasses of bark; you trail your hands over the silky paint and cold windows of the shop fronts: feel the rain on your face as your tree-self, just noticing before you shiver and wrap your scarf more closely.

Have no expectations as you remake your relationship with nature-in-the-city anew. Just be accepting of everything. Come to a crossroads and look up: the clouds have drifted whilst you walked and the first stars are shining down. It is time to be in your own home, and the scene drifts and fades like mist in a morning meadow as your senses bring you fully back in your body, feeling yourself on the chair, hearing, seeing, sensing, and smelling your everyday world and ready to pick up the threads of your life.

· · · · · · · · ·

Soon we will explore practical exercises to pursue this ultimate joining of the natural/cultural world through our artistry, our work, our craft, as recommended by Carl Jung:

> ...at any time in my later life, when I came up at a blank wall, I painted a picture or hewed stone. Each such experience proved to be a "rite d'entrée" [rite of entry] for the ideas and work that followed hard upon it.[39]

We commune with inspirited nature and ground our visions in the world of the five senses, allowing our expansive influences to enrich our lives. We stand at a balance point, bringing through the harmonious perspective of the natural world whilst fulfilling our role as fully socialised human beings.

· · · · · · · · · · ·

39 Carl Jung, *Memories, Dreams, Reflections*, trans. Clara Winston and Richard Winston, ed. Aniela Jaffe (London: Vintage-Penguin Books, 1989), 175.

Charm 9 Synopsis

❋ The ninth charm is generated by our going into the world as a co-creator. The gift from the forest is to lose preconceptions and see beauty and possibility everywhere.

❋ We follow our intuitions to embrace a wider inter-pretation of the world, every breath bonding us to the vitality of harmonizing with inspirited nature. We allow every aspect of modern culture to be included in this process.

Route Map for Charm 9

I trust the highest instincts of my heart to join the creative universe; I respect my talents; I allow time for them to emerge; I lose judgment in the join of creating; I appreciate all of my world; I thank and I record.

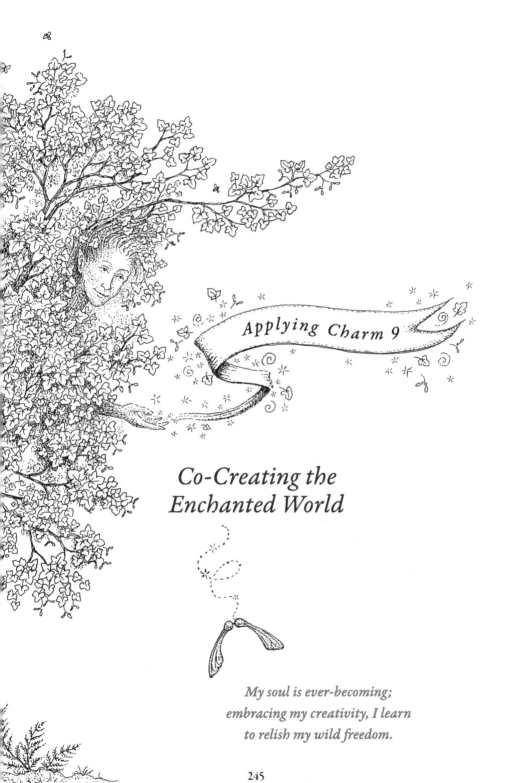

Co-Creating the
Enchanted World

*My soul is ever-becoming;
embracing my creativity, I learn
to relish my wild freedom.*

IN THIS SESSION, and whenever you revisit previous sessions, from now on, concentrate lightly—another paradox—on feeling fresh and free.

Adapt your usual morning greeting now to greet it as the Wild Day. Whilst you do this, keep an anticipatory awareness that anything could happen. Say it out loud now: "I greet the Wild Day." Does the phrase bring a rush of energy? If not, choose one that does.

The thrust of this charm is to embrace unpredictability and trust that we have the resources to deal with whatever comes. It's certainly a challenge that can be helped if we view uncertainty not as dangerous but as full of potential and ask what bright gift the day might bring.

Set an alarm at intervals through the day to remind you to reinforce this feeling until it becomes habitual. From personal experience, its optimism gives an immediate energy boost.

Our dryad's support has imbued us with an underlying understanding that we can trust life; we just have actively to do our part. As we reach out to our exciting future, we know we are more capable than we have ever believed. Soon we will be sharing all this upsurge of energy with our dryad, "telling the trees" at each stage of our adventure.

Get your journal out now and, starting with "excitement," write a list of ten emotional words associated with "wildness." I don't think the word "comfortable" will be on your list. We can have a very comfortable existence, but active, charismatic, communing living requires bravery—and the thought is exciting!

In this charm we'll learn that the boundary of our comfort zone is elastic. We do not have to jump over a firm line from comfort into fear, for fear stops us in our tracks. Instead, we gradually stretch the bounds to enter a new state of daring, backed up by what we know is reasonably achievable. We start just by doing something new, being just a little bit brave. Our dreams are usually so wonderful that "if we're this, we can't be that," says all our limiting self-talk. Nonsense. We just need to break the journey down into manageable bits. And, nine times out of ten, it will lead to a different, still wonderful place entirely! This is what we mean by holding it lightly: staying awake to all the possibilities and choosing at each stage. Can a practical IT consultant talk to a dryad? A large welder be an exquisite dancer? A hummer to the trees love stadium rock drumming? A shy person write to a famous person? A brash extrovert profess love sincerely to the beloved? Of course. Absolutely. A wild, creative spirit expands one into hitherto unknown areas, so start to practice anticipation.

Here's an interesting journal prompt: jot down now what you might do to step just out of your comfort zone. First write down what wild new ideas you would like to start exploring. Then ask: What is the simple first step to that? Then, or later, mind-map possible steps. We trust that we have only to ask for help to get it, so include how you will ask for support, from your dryad or the whole natural world, and what form it might take. Would confiding in your dryad and toasting your new venture with them remove you from human anxiety and give you confidence? Will you pledge to complete the first step within a certain timeframe as the trees witness you? And will you keep faith with that pledge?

Q: What if I fail or am embarrassed or knocked back?

A: That may happen, it might be probable, but you are not the knockback; you are the brave person who has grown by having tried; that is how we learn, and it has set you on the path to try again, in another way, very soon. Children are used to this; the only way we avoid it as adults is by never doing anything new—and that's the way back to existing, not living.

If your mind is blank at this point, there is a phrase that is helpful to embracing wild creativity; it is off the wall and funny. It is *vuja de*.[40]

Déjà vu is the strange feeling of having experienced new events before. We now programme in the opposite meaning—our sense of *vuja de*. This means seeing the familiar as if with totally fresh eyes every time, with no expectations. It can be a huge source of fun and inventiveness.[41]

We try to look with fresh eyes every time we go to our dryad. Remembering is difficult but becomes more habitual if we practice with the whole world and start with the breath. Many of us don't think about breathing; it just happens and feels like a personal, essential activity, separate from what is happening in nature. But that's wrong: every breath is dependent on what is happening around us, so we will cultivate the sense of actively breathing with our tree, and, through that, with the whole planet.[42] Or maybe, with *vuja de* understanding—for breathing happens completely automatically—we are actually, by atmosphere and gravity, being breathed? "The Earth Has Lungs. Watch Them Breathe," is the title of *National Geographic's* stunning video [43] showing the fluctuating movement of the annual CO_2 cycle of the earth and how it is affected by the seasons. Watch it to encourage and guide your own imagining.

Then, holding an awareness of the whole breathing planet, we'll join the sentient world—choose a fine day, as we need a suggestion of sun on the leaves—with some tree breathing.

· · · · · · · · · · · ·

40 See https://advice.theshineapp.com/articles/forget-deja-vu-vuja-de-is -the-mindful-hack-you-need/ (accessed November 2021).

41 An example of *vuja de* by Joss Whedon resulted in the TV series *Buffy the Vampire Slayer*, turning the horror genre on its head by making the pretty blonde the aggressor, not the victim: all monsters are her prey.

42 Rudolf Steiner, an Austrian philosopher, educator, and agriculturalist (1861–1925), wrote extensively on the daily and annual breathing cycle of the earth.

43 Robert Krulwich, "The Earth Has Lungs. Watch Them Breathe," *National Geographic* (8 March 2016), https://www.nationalgeographic .com/science/phenomena/2016/03/09/the-earth-has-lungs-watch -them-breathe/ (accessed October 2020).

Breathing with the Landscape

Start at a distance to your tree so that you can view it comfortably. Say hello to your dryad; you will be closer very soon. We will concentrate on our dryad's leaves today. Choose a place where you can most easily imagine air cycling between you. Allow your breath to come naturally and set your focal point beyond your tree to sense its energy field, a pulse in its aura. You do not have to see with your physical eyes. Today, interpret that pulse, however you perceive it, as your tree breathing just as you do: taking in life-giving oxygen and breathing out CO_2 through its leaves. All living creatures respire. Feel the process in your own lungs; focus on your diaphragm, your nostrils, as you count the air in and out your lungs in your own comfortable rhythm, two living creatures breathing together.

After a few cycles, the leaves call your attention. Each breathing leaf is also transpiring, exhaling water, thereby cooling and refreshing the atmosphere. Sense at your nostrils the damp freshness imbuing the air. You are fortified and calmed by it as you breathe with this focus.

Become aware of the sun, its rays striking the leaves and enabling them to photosynthesise—to manufacture food from CO_2 and water. The byproduct of this is oxygen: sense it vitalising the air in a heady rush with each inbreath. Continue to breath steadily.

In your mind's eye, view all these processes as rainbow colours in a constant gracious movement meeting the processes of other trees, humans, dogs, life forms... You might assign colours to the different gases and water vapour as they interact. Allow CO_2 to blow from your outbreath, to be taken up by your dryad; see miniscule water vapour droplets fountaining down around you and the constant stream of oxygen flowing over all.

If it feels right, continue the exercise as you walk to your tree to breathe consciously with your dryad, connecting physically by leaning, stroking, sitting. Breathe in the wild idea that time is on your side; that you can be still and witness; that new ideas will flow up and invigorate you to creative action; that you are moving into your true, authentic, joined-up self.

How does that feel? Lighter, energised? Where is the feeling located: the head, the heart, the pelvis, somewhere else? Think of it as a nut of deep wisdom that you hold within. It has sweetness, nourishment, and potential to grow a whole tree. And how many other nuts will your tree-self produce? Embrace the wildness and possibility of this question.

As you return to the world of everyday with thanks, make simple notes immediately of thoughts, feelings, and impressions that seem significant. Memories from liminal space are so easily overwhelmed that they must be captured without delay.

• • • • • • • • •

Our next experience will be hands-on-creative. There is most material for it in the autumn/fall, but any time of year provides plenty that nature has discarded for us to assemble thoughtfully and make a thing of beauty. We've made simple natural gifts, twisted from grasses and seeds, and now we progress to more formed natural art. This is planned but ephemeral—gone with the wind and the natural trickle of life. It may pinpoint a particular time and experience to witness or commemorate or it may be for the joy in the making. There are many examples in books and on the internet to inspire us.[44] One of the leaders in this field is Andy Goldsworthy, famous for ephemeral nature art, whose breathtaking gradations of colour in the simplest leaf collage amaze and excite.

• • • • • • • • • • • •

44 For example, the books *Wood, Leaves, Stones,* and *Time,* all by Andy Goldsworthy (see bibliography).

Do not be overwhelmed by his mastery! You can achieve something unique within a few minutes, and will have learnt by doing. From my first personal experience, it was to thread leaf stems together to stop them blowing away even as I put them down. Each few minutes that you try will teach you something new.

Dedicate the time needed, settle into the zone, and ask that the wildness of the genius loci pay attention, draw near, and bless your work. Feel the otherness of the breeze on your neck; the encouragement of the pigeon and squirrel. By adding your contribution to nature's beauty, you are paying the respect of your regard and attention to the local nature spirits. By going out of your comfort zone to do it and getting over all your initial reactions (viz: "I'm rubbish, I'll look ridiculous, my results will be embarrassingly bad ... "), you are growing your sense of yourself. Set your intent. Trust. I think your dryad will be very proud of you. I think you will go home feeling proud of yourself. One of my first attempts was not particularly good, but the point is, I did it—and I was spurred on by examples from a student far more competent than I am.

When you've finished and photographed or sketched your results, stay a moment with art and *vuja de*. Forget your limitations as you allow your capabilities to reveal themselves.

Ask yourself where your dryad might direct you next. Look around: what riches are freely available from nature at the moment? Listen; is something floating as an idea? What wants to be created, and where? Be a nature spotter. Suppose that all your creative instincts had to be channeled through natural, found objects. How many could you find?

The wonder of art is in making
us slow down and step aside from
our usual view of things and their
relationships to our lives. We
embrace a richer sense of reality.

Read that sentence again, carefully, with this slight change: "The wonder of *charming our dryad* is in making us slow down and step aside from our usual view of things and their relationships to our lives. We embrace a richer sense of reality."

So is all we've been doing art? Yes. Working imaginatively with the world in thought, visualisation, or in whatever form is an art. Maybe every time we go to our dryad we are living our lives as an art form. We understand nature by being a part of it—just as transient, just as beautiful, just as much an essential part of the whole.

Consider yourself as a kinetic art form—walking, running through the landscape. Your presence in the landscape is an interactive artistic experience, regardless of the result. Make art to connect you to the land—a crown, a sash, a garter, necklace, or bracelet. Remember the childhood days of daisy chains: bring one to your tree to crown a bough.[45] Land art, sand and ice sculptures, pressing leaves into clay, and chalk drawings are all examples of ephemeral art. You probably experimented with all of them in play when you were a child. Time to relearn!

And now back to sharing the breath of the first trees and ancestors through that constant gas, argon. We find the second connection in cave art worldwide, from the Stone Age onward. The urge to create has been hard-wired into our species: it is an expression of life that we carry and act on in our turn. Art history reveals our glorious inheritance. Consider: if we restricted ourselves to natural resources, how different would our body and decorative art be from that of our ancestors? Their ephemeral art would have looked remarkably similar to ours, I suspect.

Visual art may not be your thing, but do this in the spirit of carrying our heritage forward, overlooked by the tree spirits just as our forebears were. And then adapt and move into your own creative area—movement, sound, slide guitar, or cake decorations. Just keep going back to nature for your inspiration.

. . . .

45 Readers are aware of environmental issues, protected species, and so on, so only act responsibly. Nature's bounty dictates our choice and we ask the plants before picking, of course.

You will doubtless have days feeling uninspired, and the advice, like argon, remains constant to activate your fascination and attention. Greet wild inventiveness. Don't look inward; look out, as Tim Brown says:

> I've always believed that I can't be creative unless I'm inspired in some way. Inspiration is a funny thing; it sounds like it's an internal thing. We think of great creative artists and imagine that inspiration wells up inside of them, but I think that's just not true. *Inspiration comes from the outside. The most inspirational people are the most observant people who are able to take from the outside world and convert what they see into something that drives their creativity. The simplest and most effective way of doing that is to notice things*...[46] (my italicizing)

Now, as we walk, we will take our creative instincts and run wild with them. On every walk, make a strong intention to think out of the box and encourage stray, random, and lateral thoughts that you might generally dismiss as silly. Be curious, diverted; expect the unusual and cultivate a sense of, and joy for, the surreal.

Suppose you could never leave the house without first knotting a silk string around your neck. Bizarre? But a million men would never go out without a tie... it's all in the way you look at our accepted habits. With *vuja de* we look with the eyes of a child—and, as in fairy tales, we may find we've been hoodwinked into accepting an emperor with no clothes on!

Send word ahead to your dryad for help, and use these affirmations:

🌿 Every step leads me to my dryad, who will support
   my wild inventiveness.

🌿 I generate as many ideas as there are leaves on the tree.

—and believe what you are saying.

. . . .

46 Helen Walters, "The World's Best Creative Director: Nature," Ideas.Ted.
   Com (7 Febuary 2014), https://ideas.ted.com/nature-knows-best
   -a-biologist-and-a-designer-take-creative-direction-from-the-earths
   -operating-system/ (accessed September 2020).

•EXERCISE•

Thinking the Unexpected

Take your journal to your tree and use your preferred method of centring down to evoke your tree-ness and connect to your dryad.

Prime your *vuja de* by considering wild thoughts:

- Suppose nourishment travelled down the tree into the roots to go into the earth?

- Suppose the leaves were blue and the sky green?

- Suppose trees cocked their branches at passing dogs and showered them with sap?

- Suppose energy lines were like bungee cords and could swing us up to the tree canopy?

- Suppose that oval scar on the trunk morphed into a doorway; what would appear? Where would we end up if we stepped inside?

- Suppose people were rooted and trees and hedges walked?

Now think of as many again of your own—as ridiculous as you wish, so aim to make yourself smile.

Scribble, jot, sketch, have fun ... allow time to become more still. Gently pose your desired question and ask for possibilities to emerge. Sink into the green and dream wild, no holds barred, and note every suggestion in your journal. If unicorns and puppies appear, so be it: no judgment, no critical faculty restricts you. A lot may be nonsensical; some will be irresponsible: that's okay, as this is a list to free your mind, not act on. Take your results home, look at them periodically, and prime your mind before sleep to work on creative solutions that you can actually put into practice.

It is time to go back to our everyday world now, and by the same close observation that we have used in nature, we exponentially increase our intuitive faculty.

As we instinctively gravitated to the right tree, so we will start to "read" our social and professional group in the same way: we become more sensitive to ambience. It may already be happening, and you'll find that "people reading" makes Zoom meetings more interesting. Practice on your next trip to town or the hypermarket. We are bombarded by twenty-first-century commerce with its sound, colour, animations, adverts, Muzak, and so on... Which is most pervasive, which grating, which seductive? Observe closely the effects of the mall, the market, the club, the coffee shop. Take a break for a coffee and to make notes; if you get overloaded, take your journal to the peace of the park.

Q: How, in light of your charming experiences, do you want to arrange your life/society and life/nature balance? Does it need adjusting? How might you do that?

A: Little and gently... which activities can be reduced, which encouraged?

Q: Isn't it callous to distance ourselves from nice people who don't support or are closed to our new way of thinking?

A: Are you overestimating your importance? If you gently, kindly loosen ties, you are freeing up their time for their more productive relationships with people more in tune with them.

Lastly, for we have a whole glorious world to rejoin, let us sink into just being a part of nature.

> *We are not "in nature," we*
> *are nature: walking, talking*
> *expressions of nature.*

So, let's end by describing ourselves with reference to that nature, not to humanity. This was commonplace in early writings of an earthly beloved, for when the arts were always of religious subjects, nature was the only point of comparison that wasn't blasphemous.

For almost the last time in this stage of your study, gather up your journal. Go to the mirror. Forget supermodel A, pop star B, and film star C; airbrushed perfection manufactures their images, making them irrelevant. No one can duplicate our own brilliant uniqueness—crooked teeth, noble nose, laughter lines, smiling eyes and all.

As you look in the mirror, by some double-exposure trickery, can you imagine the natural world mirrored in you? If you've worked your way through the book, it is truly deep within. We are each our own beloved, and beloved of our dryad, so let's describe ourselves as such. Write a praise poem to yourself; you've been practising on your dryad. Look dispassionately as if at a stranger you feel immense attraction to. This person intrigues you. How can you describe them?

Use only natural images: is your hair spiky gorse or smooth wheat, a fountain, streaming ivy, a waterfall? Is your shaven head a hill in winter? Your breast white as the swan, soft as a rabbit, firm as teak? Skin dark as the raven, tawny and freckled as an owl's wing, glossy as the horse chestnut? Are your eyes pools or stars in the abalone sky of your irises? Does your face glow like the sun? Is the curve of your shoulder like the slope of a hill? Is the curve of your body under the duvet like a landscape? Your voice like a brook, a breeze, a linnet, the cawing of a rook? Take your time and add to this over several days.

I believe that making these comparisons with the natural world will allow your relationship with yourself to shift subtly. Do it faithfully and see. Record everything you notice in your journal.

What could be more potent than the simplicity of Robert Burns's

O my Luve is like a red, red rose
That's newly sprung in June... [47]

Or Dafydd ap Gwilym's praise of a beauty called Morfudd:

... she is radiant,
And brighter than a crest of foam
White as the glistening, garrulous wave's edge,
With the Sun's splendour... [48]

Poets, overflowing with love, connect the universe and the beloved, to whom they say, "You are my world."

And we are saying, with love, "you are my world" to the whole world—the trees, our local nature spirits, and the communicating eco-structure that binds us to the whole. So let us celebrate humanity as sweet tender shoots; of our babies, our sapling adolescents, our adults with hearts of oak, our wise ones like ancient trees. Our nature, flowing free, is sweet as fruit, potential-full as a nut; our spirits range free through the entire cosmos at will, stroking the world with fingers delicate as twigs, rooting strongly in times of stress, allowing the flexibility of the willow in the gale.

Our loving companions—human,
animal, tree, river, stone—glow
with moon and starlight and shine
bright as the sun, and so do we.

· · · · · · · · · · · ·

47 Robert Burns, "A Red, Red Rose," https://www.poetryfoundation.org /poems/43812/a-red-red-rose (accessed May 2020).

48 Daffyd ap Gwilym, *Selected Poems of Daffyd ap Gwilym*, trans. Rachel Bromwich (Harmondsworth: Penguin, 1985), 26.

When we can reframe and reference our world in this way, we may begin to think of ourselves as lovers of the world, walkers in the woods, charmers of dryads.

Whenever you have time, sink again into the green dreaming to allow your true nature-self to arise as an image to bring into reality. Use every medium you reasonably can—paint, collage, photography, sgraffito, glazing; adding pressed leaves, ink from earth or fruits, stuck-on seeds and fibres. Start collecting your materials on your next walk whilst your ideas are still in flux. The strengths and weaknesses of the natural materials will guide the direction you take.

Q: How to portray yourself? What qualities have you been gifted by your dryad? Which come from the trees of your childhood?

A: Your choice of tree spirit name and type will depend on where you live or your cultural heritage. Do you see within yourself a dryad, Druid ("wood wisdom"), Kodama, Lauma, Apple Tree Man, wood nymph, Yashshina, or Tapio with his beard of lichen and eyebrows of moss— or tree spirit from any other part of the globe?

Will your image show your inner self in the guise of a green man/woman, a representative of the genius loci, or spirit of the greenwood? From the British Isles we have Puck, Robin Hood, Marion of Sherwood, and Merlin, but you will know the names of those that live in the memory of your own land.

Plan, think, let all your senses have an impact. This is one picture that can truly be called conceptual art. Thought, feeling, sight, smell, taste, and hearing will all have had their input.

Evoke your authentic, natural self and trust your picture to reveal your unique, wild, free, human spirit. Shine like a tree, like a dryad, as you make your way through the world.

To charm our dryad, to bring a new
relationship into being, is a supreme
creative act and one that can bring
us a lifetime of joyous revelation.

Let us wake every morning to these questions:

❦ How will my magical tree relationship manifest
   today?

❦ What forms will my creativity and thankfulness take?

❦ What expression will the wild, exciting day ask of me?

May our artistry, whatever form it takes, help spread the enchantment of
the trees through the everyday world for the good of all beings.

Conclusion

A Letter from the Forest to the Walker in the Woods

Come live with me through my seasons, imbibing the nourishment of nature.

The earth, air, water, and fire of the sun will support, invigorate, cleanse, and vitalise you through all of your days. They may burn, drench, blow at, and trip you so that you feel you are losing your way in the forest, but always the elements are reflected in your body as bone, breath, blood, and energy. When you accept the totality of their nourishment—the sweet of the nectar, the astringent bitterness of herbs—as essential, you will take your place as Walker in the Woods. You will belong.

You know deep inside that, like your dryad, you are an essence, a life force within a physical body. Paradoxically, you are simultaneously not as significant as your ego may always have fought to believe: and yet, much more significantly, you are truly unique and necessary to the world at this time. You contain everything that you need, and you take your proper place in the world.

Like your tree kin, you belong on this magical living planet that sustains more profound needs than those of the physical body. Just by walking thoughtfully, respectfully, and accepting whatever you may receive, you are joining the worlds of matter and spirit within yourself through communion with other inspired inhabitants of our miraculous planet.

Walk in my forest through the seasons; you are a mirror for our world.

Winter: The Evergreen Speaks

I sleep, secure in my world. Deep within my being is my dormant soul … Like a bear, I hibernate; I maintain, I stand amid the icy weather, the gales, the sleet, as stoically as I will stand in the parched time of great heat. Walker in the Woods, witness my strength, my height; I am a far seer. Be still and witness with me, poised and pregnant before the dance recommences. Do I glimpse spring on the far horizon? My enduring leaves are my promise that spring will return to green the world again. I am pine, eucalyptus, South African yellowwood, and I am in the equatorial forest whose temperature has no understanding of winter …

My dreaming sweetens the winter air. What loving messages will you breathe into my bark to float on the wind from me to your distant loved ones? How will you dance with your dryad through the winter? Whisper to me, infuse my dreams with your longings, and be strengthened in your turn.

Spring: The Voice of the Birch

I am awakening! The light grows, and enchantment transforms the world. My roots love the damp loam, and water, light, and sun send an imperative message to me … My catkins, the flowers that have been in stasis through the cold, grow long and tremble in the warming breezes. My flowers hang straight like a shower of green rain held by a magician's spell on the twig. Sap pours to the tip of every bud and flows in abundance to bless my body; like my cousin the maple, when it runs I can gift it plentifully, giving sweet sap to revitalise the human tribe, the clan, my distant relations. My leaves are clear green spears; my flowers hang, shake, disperse their pollen to the wind, dusting the earth, marking your forehead as you duck beneath my hanging boughs, marking you, Walker in the Woods, as tree kin.

Summer: The Expansion of the Oak

I am awake! Mine were not the first leaves to appear. I have taken my time to unfurl each precious green gift. And I saw you, Walker in the Woods, encouraging me in the spring, your body poised like a curled leaf, as you too became a bud in your dance through the year. And now my strength pours out to bless the world—the insects, animals, and birds who find life in me, the people refreshed by my shade and my cooler, fragrant atmosphere. I am a king and queen tree, and as you rest under me, Walker in the Woods, feel sovereign of yourself. Stretch and loosen your joints, allowing life to flood through unimpeded to fill your heart. Firm and pliant in the storms, my twigs may thrash, but my great trunk endures; bearing the scar of the lightning strike of inspiration, I still endure. Like your scars, it is a badge of life to wear—a part of me. By standing tall, you allow others to stand. Supporting, you are open to allow support when you need it. Past midsummer I will flush again with new leaflets to greet the ripening sun; so will you grow in strength at every time of your life.

Autumn: The Fruiting of the Nut

I am warm ripeness. Call me almond, beech, hazel, hickory, macadamia, pistachio, sweet chestnut, walnut—I am your neighbour, and my twigs bend with nuts, their casing browning into ripeness: nature's bounty for all the world.

The magic of the season transforms the forests, making a glorious spectacle of reds, oranges, and yellows. The green rain of the hanging spring flowers has transformed into an organic sunset-splendour of dying leaves. Falling gently to form an exquisite carpet of copper, bronze, and gold, they patter like autumn rain to delight you. As the leaves rustle around your feet, feel your true harvest of love and achievement.

Cast off the outworn, all those things that had their beauty but whose time is gone, and go forward singing! Be the sweet kernel of the nuts of wisdom. Hold safe within you all you have learnt from your year in the forest. Gather my nuts as you gather the berries and fruits of my kindred plants. You are as welcome as all the wild creatures: and of them all, only you, Walker in the Woods, might imbibe consciously the potential held by each one: the concentration of intent stored in each nutrient-rich package.

The fallow time approaches. Without space and time, no new thing of worth can arise. Store my fruits to sustain you as you gently wind down with the natural cycle.

• • • • • • • • •

And now the whispering breeze carries the voice of the genius loci, the spirit of the woods. Listen closely.

The deep woods are my sanctum sanctorum; they are my repository of stored sunlight, a living, breathing temple of life. The perfection of the trees gleams with precious metals reflected from the sun, moon, and stars.

As night turns to day, gleaming silver strips of light highlight gnarled tree trunks and high boughs.

At dawn the light gleams through the electrum green of the spring leaves.

At midday the leafy veil of the high summer sun bathes us in brazen green-gold shafts of light.

The autumn sunset turns my deepest places into a treasure house spilling over with copper and bronze.

At winter's eve I rest with the pewter and rust of the forest floor, the exquisite traceries of black wire twigs high against the sky.

I am the spirit of the forest clearing, and you may rest, imbibing green vitality, breathing my health-giving odours, drinking the sun, soothed by my shadows, whenever you wish.

Like me, you will be crowned by the forest light, for I am just a thought away.

Acknowledgments

Thanks, first and foremost, to the Holm Oak and Yew of the quiet cloister: the Linden and Plane of the park, the Ash and Elm of the stream—and all our gracious leaved and long-lived cousins.

Next, to the Druid students and friends who have joined me in testing out the visualisations and discussing ideas; and especial gratitude to Druid colleagues Marion, Pia, and Tanya, whose generosity in sharing their experiences made possible the appendix on ill health and mobility issues.

To all who have helped the evolution of my tree consciousness, especially the Order of Bards, Ovates and Druids.

To the nature writers and ecologists whose intuitive faculties and sensitised interpretation of scientific findings stretch the boundaries and allow us all to grow.

To my family, as always: rarely acknowledged, always essential, forever loved.

And lastly, thanks to Elysia, Becky, and all at Llewellyn for their continued enthusiasm, professionalism, and support.

Appendix 1

Dryads from Classical Myth

Our earliest dryad stories are from the ancient Greeks, so here is a brief compilation of those that have come down to us. The Greeks' definition of dryads was that they are nymph-like tree spirits who could leave their parent tree temporarily. Hamadryads, by comparison, are the spirit of the tree, completely a part of its physical presence and unable to leave.

A further dryad classification is by region:

Oreiades were the conifers of the forested mountains.

Alseides were trees of the sacred groves.

Aulonides and Napaiai were of the glens and valleys.

Greek Dryads by Tree and Story

Almond Tree—Phyllis, a Thracian princess, died waiting for her lover Acamas to return from Troy. She was metamorphosed by Athene into an almond tree. Acamas arrived the next day and embraced the tree, whereupon the branches burst into flower instead of leaf, a habit of almond trees ever since.

Apple and Fruit Trees—The Maliades, Meliades, or Epimelides were nymphs of the apple tree and protectors of flocks of sheep and goats, as *melas* means both apple and sheep. They were the guardians of the golden fleece (see also Oak), and include the famous Hesperides (see Apples, Golden).

Apples, Golden, of Immortality—As a magical fruit, these apples hold several dryad stories and were guarded by dryads. The trees of the Golden Apples of Immortality were a wedding gift from the goddess Gaia to Hera. The Hesperides who guard them are three dryads also called the Daughters of the Evening (father: the Titan Atlas) or the Daughters of Night (parents: Nyx, the night, and Erebus, darkness). Their orchard is in the far west, the place of sunset; *Hesperos* means evening, and Hesperus is the evening star, Venus. Their names are Aigle (dazzling light), Erytheia, and Hesperia (sunset glow). The most famous legend of the Apples of Immortality is of Eris, goddess of discord, offering one to the Trojan Paris to give as a prize to the goddess he judged most beautiful. Aphrodite, goddess of love, promised him Helen of Troy and so caused the Trojan War.

Ash Tree—Meliae. The ash dryads were born when blood from the castration of the Titan Uranus (grandfather of the Olympian gods) fertilised the earth mother, Gaia. Zeus, the chief of the Olympian gods, was nursed by dryads of the ash tree on Crete. In the most ancient times, they were married to men, and we have all descended from them.

Black Poplar—Nymphai Aigeiroi. When the young Phaeton was killed trying to drive the chariot of the sun god, the gods transformed his grieving sisters in black poplars.

Cherry Tree Dryads—Kraneiai

Elm Dryads—Pteleai

Figs—Sykei

Fir Dryad—Pitys was turned into a fir tree to escape from Pan, after which he wore a branch of fir as a chaplet.

Grapevine Dryads—Ampeloi

Hamadryads—Although some sources say they were unable to leave their trees, several notable hamadryads obviously did. Here are three references from ancient stories:

> Dryope (woodpecker/oak face) the daughter of Dryops (oak). She was seduced by Apollo and became a priestess until the hamadryads

stole her away, leaving a poplar in her place. She lived in Arcadia and gave birth to Pan, whose father might have been Zeus, king of the gods, Dionysus, the god of fertility and wine, or Hermes. Pan (meaning "all" or "everything") predates the compartmentalised roles of the later gods.

Dryope and her sisters enticed away Herakles' lover, Hylas, to live with them in an underwater grotto. Many parallel stories accrued round the names of famous dryads.

Chrysopeleia's dwelling tree was in danger from a flooding river. She was rescued by Arcas, who was hunting nearby and who saved her tree with a dam that altered the river's flow. Chrysopeleia bore him two sons.

Ilex (Holly)—Balanis

Hazel nut—Karyai (see Walnut)

Laurels—Daphnae. Eros, god of infatuated love, having been insulted by Apollo, cursed him to pursue Daphne, daughter of a river god. Fleeing, she appealed to her father, who changed her into a laurel tree, but Apollo still loved and embraced her; he held the laurel in high regard from that time. Laurel crowns were awarded to the winners of athletic/cultural competitions, and this continues to the present day.

Mulberry—Moreai

Oak and Poplars—The Hamadryads, often associated with sacred groves. The Golden Fleece, won by Jason, was hung on an oak in a grove (see also Apple), guarded with bulls, trumpets, and a sleeping dragon.

Pine Tree—Oreiades. The dryads of the conifers have a long lineage. The earliest were daughters of the Daktyloi, an ancient race of men coming from the Great Mother, and the Hekaterides, the nymphs of dance; their brothers were the satyrs. Pitys (also attributed to the fir) was pursued by Pan and was changed by the gods into a pine to escape him.

Reed—Syrinx was pursued by Pan from Mt. Lynaeum to the River Ladon, where she was changed into a reed. As he couldn't distinguish her from the others, Pan cut a bundle at random and turned them into a panpipe. Hermes copied the pipe, claimed it as his own invention, and sold it to Apollo.

Walnut Trees—Karyatids (Caryatids). Karya was the daughter of the king of Laconia, gifted with prophecy by Apollo. Dionysus loved her, and after her death he changed her into a walnut tree (in some versions, a hazel). The Laconians built a temple to Artemis Karyatis, and the Karyatids, dedicated to Artemis, for whom they danced with baskets of living reeds in their native town of Karyai.

Dryad Family

Of the dryads on the list above, these are sisters:

Karya, the walnut dryad; Morea of the mulberry; Kraneia, dogwood; Balanis, ilex or oak; Aigeiros, black poplar; Ptelea, elm; Ampelos, vines; and Syke, fig, were the eight daughters of Oxylus, the result of an incestuous union with his sister Hamadryas.

Named dryads in story—trees unknown:

Eurydice—Eurydice was a dryad, nymph of trees and woodlands, married to Orpheus, the son of Apollo, who taught him how to play the lyre. Eurydice died of a snake bite soon after her wedding. Orpheus ventured into Hades for her, quietening the three-headed guard dog Kerberus with his music, and brought her out. But he disobeyed the god's prohibition and turned to look at her, and she was forced to return to the underworld.

Erato—"lovely, desired." Erato was a priestess of Pan, with prophetic verses attributed to her at an ancient oracle of the god at Megalopolis. She was the wife of Arcas (see charm 7), the son of Zeus and Callisto, and was the muse of lyric poetry.

Appendix 2

From Greece to Britain:
Groves, Oracles, and Ancient Tree Ritual

Greece

Details of actual Greek rituals to honour dryads is rare. We know that long-lived tree spirits exerted a very real influence and that ceremonies of appeasement were necessary before cutting to prevent punishment by the gods, who protected them. The theory for the rarity of references to these rituals is that they would have been too well known to need reporting. But we do know a little about one oracle, and there are stories of using wood from oracular trees.

The oak oracle of Dodona was dedicated to Zeus. Supplicating the oracle involved prayers, and during the oracle ritual, priestesses would sing a hymn in praise of great Zeus and the Earth Mother. Questions were written on tablets, sometimes with the answers written on the back. At the goddess Athene's instigation, a piece of sacred oak was carved and placed in the ship Argo and would talk to Jason and the Argonauts. The sacred oak of Dodona was cut and the shrine abandoned around 391 CE, when the Emperor Theodosius banned all Pagan practices, replacing the old religion with Christianity.

The Grove of Selloi was comprised of oak and beech trees. In the tragedy "Women of Trachis," Sophocles tells us that any tree in it could prophecy through the rustling of their leaves. That sound was increased by hanging brass cans on their branches, and the sounds were interpreted by their priestesses.

The temple of Delphi, dedicated to Apollo, was the preeminent oracular site in ancient Greece. It was believed that the god lived within a laurel, and the oracle was interpreted from the rustling of its leaves via his priestess, the Pythia, after a ritual purification ceremony in a sacred spring and drinking of the waters.

Oracular trees and groves were an important part of the religious culture of the ancient world, as evidenced by the significant distances they travelled for a prophecy and the high status of the personnel who consulted the gods in this way.

Britain

Northern Europe was heavily forested at the time of the flowering of the Greek culture that produced the stories of the dryads. We might consider that folklore is the remnant of ancient belief in tree spirits from this time, for, alas, there are no written records until the Romans conquered and reported on the tree rituals of the Druids.

The Greeks and Romans tell us that the branch of Druids called Uates (present-day Ovates) particularly studied the high mysteries of nature. Their rituals took place in sacred groves, always with a representative piece of oak.

As Britain was at the far reaches of the known world to the Greeks and Romans, it is amazing that we do have one complete tree ritual from those times, recorded by Pliny in the *Naturalis Historia* from 77 CE: the only complete account from the islands whose trees have inspired this work.

Can we doubt that this ritual is the culmination of the Druids' dryad charming, of having a living relationship and obtaining through ritual the blessings of a magical plant, nurtured on their most sacred tree?

The Druid Mistletoe Ritual

Here we must mention the awe felt for this plant by the Gauls. The Druids—for so their magicians are called—held nothing more sacred than the mistletoe and the tree that bears it, always supposing that tree to be the oak. But they choose grooves formed off hooks for the sake of the tree alone, and they never perform any of their rights except in the presence of a branch of it; so that it seems probable that the priests may derive their name from the Greek word for that tree. In fact they think that everything that grows on it has been sent from heaven and is a proof that the tree was chosen by the god himself. The mistletoe, however is found that really upon the oak; and when found, is gathered with due religious ceremony, if possible, on the sixth day of the moon brackets for it is by the moon that they measure of the months and years, and also the ages of 30 years). They choose this day because the moon, not yet in the middle of her course, has already considerable influence. They called the mistletoe by a name meaning in their language, the all healing. Having made preparation for sacrifice and a banquet beneath the trees, they bring thither two white bulls, whose horns are bound then for the first time. Clad in a white robe, the priest sends the tree and cuts the mistletoe with a golden circle, and it is received by others in a white cloak.

When they kill the victims, praying that God will render this gift of his pride precious to those to whom he has granted it. They believe that the mistletoe, taken in drink, imports fecundity to Barren animals and that it is an antidote for all poisons. Such are the religious feelings that are entertained towards trifling things by many people.—Pliny (23–79 CE), *Historia Naturalis*, XVI, 249 [49]

49 John Matthews, editor, *The Druid Source Book* (London: Brockhampton Press, 1998), 21. Reprinted with kind permission.

Appendix 3

The Sacred Nature of Trees

Throughout human history trees have been revered for their sacred nature. Trees have always represented a conduit to a spirit, a divine wisdom, which we harmonise with through intuitive, formal, or ritual acts. For dryad charmers, this is the background every time we pick a fruit. We are accepting a gift from a vital and sentient life force and sharing spiritual connection with a greater spirit.

Trees are the meeting place of the realms of matter and spirit, and many religious buildings emulate the forest—the first temples of the gods. Foliage grows on columns and strange faces emerge from the carvings on cathedrals; stained glass makes a dappled light like that of a grove; pillars soar like pine and yew trunks. Trees are represented everywhere.

By developing customs, we contribute to this joining of the human and tree kingdom for the good of all beings.

Customs

Customs arise around groves and specific trees to show their specific sacred nature, especially in the centre of human habitations or on boundaries. The Gospel Oak area of Camden in northwest London is named for the tree under which people congregated to hear gospel readings. It marked the boundary between Hampstead and Saint Pancras until the early 1800s.

The incontestable link between trees and the divine is clearly shown by the stories of saints who demonstrated their holiness by cutting down a sacred tree whose worship predated Christianity, such as St. Boniface, who felled Donar's Oak in Germany. During the English Civil War many ancient sacred trees—regarded as focuses for Catholic idolatry and superstition[50]— were felled. In Europe, home of venerable trees, those important to village cultures were often rededicated to the Virgin and Christian saints. They continue their role for communities to this day, and their future is nurtured by local inhabitants.[51]

Legal Witnesses

Trees have a significant status of providing a space and witness to legally binding contracts. Amazingly, in the UK, one is still living from those times. The 30-feet-wide, 2,500-year-old Ankerwycke yew was already an ancient tree in 1215 when the famous Magna Carta between King John and his barons was signed. A charming British legend says that beneath the 900-year-old yew in St. Cuthbert's churchyard, Doveridge, Derbyshire, Robin Hood and Maid Marion "plighted their troth." And all over Central Europe, the most venerable tree in many towns and villages became a site of justice where the visiting magistrate sat in judgment.

In the United States there is an initiative to mark trees that have witnessed significant moments in history—for example, the Battle of Gettysburg—and one stated reason is the thrill of communing with an ancient living witness rather than an inanimate object. We dryad charmers agree.

. . . .

50 English Civil War (Roundheads v. Cavaliers, 1642–51). Example: The Puritan felling of the Glastonbury Thorn (supposedly a miraculous planting by Joseph of Arimathea) as a superstitious relic of Catholicism. Legend says that the feller was blinded by a flying splinter. Replacements were planted, the latest having been hacked down within the last few years.

51 There are too many wonderful stories to relate here, enough to warrant a "European tree of the year" competition. One nice example concerns the 500-year-old "Venerable Oak" in Novo Selo village, Bulgaria: locals planted a small oak tree by it in 2010 so it would learn and carry on the witnessed story of "The Old Man" when, in due course, he succumbs to the ravages of time.

Totem Trees

Totem trees are seen to carry part of the spirit of a community, and to injure them is to cut to its heart—rather like disrespecting or damaging a country's flag. The totem tree of Carmarthen, Merlin's oak, had its legend attached as "when Merlin's oak shall tumble down, then shall fall Carmarthen town." Two modern examples of the investment we still have in totem trees would be the furious reaction to the vandalising of the Auburn University oaks in the US and the malicious chopping down of the Glastonbury thorn in the UK. There is no doubt that both communities were deeply wounded by these actions.

Every major city has its landmark ancient trees that have taken on the mantle as icons, and we see this also in the associations of many Scottish clans and in at least five European countries that have the lime, or linden, as their national tree and hold it sacred. A moment's thought will connect other countries to their national trees: the oak to England, the US, and Germany; maple to Canada; birch to Finland and Sweden; banyan to India; olive to Israel; willow to the Ukraine, and the palm to Saudi Arabia.

As dryad charmers, we may forge our own unique connection between a tree genus and our own family and locality. Some of us will have lived with this understanding as background to all our lives.

Life Rites

The symbolism of the tree connects it intimately with our life rites. Their life cycle echoes ours and sets our significant events into a wider context. They join the worlds of sky and earth. They live, as we do, through an alchemy that fuses the four elements into living matter: they are reminders of peace and continuity.

In supporting the modern wish for spiritual rather than religious life rites, trees are the perfect mediators. Ceremonies are held under a sacred tree in a grove or especially designated areas of woodland. It is common to plant a tree to commemorate a birth, death, or significant event. Woodland burials are increasingly popular, and it is wonderful to see open land gradually become healthy mixed woodland, each tree a living memory of a loved one.

Weddings and relationship commitment ceremonies of all kinds are frequently held in woodland; the quiet atmosphere of "nature's cathedral" holds gravitas and life energy that infuses any ritual, with our wise tree relations witnessing our vows.

So, specifically, we might—

❋ Plant a tree for a new birth. In rural areas of the UK, a stand of willow trees would be planted on the birth of a girl. When the time came for her to be married, selling the trees to make cricket bats would pay for the wedding.

❋ Dedicate a tree to a baby, with the feeling that a tree will in some way "sponsor" the child through life.

❋ Hold a baby naming (instead of christening) in woodland.

❋ Plant a new tree in the garden over the placenta.

❋ Have a woodland wedding. In Switzerland newlyweds plant a pine tree after the ceremony to symbolise fertility and bring good luck.

❋ Make private vows of all kinds, witnessed by the trees.

❋ Have a woodland burial. In Zurich, forests close to cemeteries have communal trees for several urns or family trees rented for thirty years (or an undefined period).

❋ Buy a tree as a memorial.

❋ Sponsor a tree at any significant life transition through organisations such as the Woodland Trust.

❋ Give gifts to the family tree as thanks.

❋ "Tell the trees"—share your family news (exam results, births, deaths, hopes and fears) with them to build relationship.

Trees have always been useful to nomadic peoples especially as a focus for passing judgments and holding rituals, and we nature spirituality students can be confident that when we hug, kiss, or leave an offering of fruit or water to a tree, we are part of an honourable lineage. Ancient tribespeople have done it all before and for the same reasons.

Appendix 4

A Year of Tree Customs

ollowing tree custom and tradition is a practical way of developing a balanced, gentle approach to the turning year. Seasonal tree customs arise from an ongoing relationship—at harvest times especially—and are embedded in the history of our locality. We can bring those back into use or allow new ones to arise. All our customs should be living, meaning they are relevant, valuable, and built into the fabric of life. An example of a personal event might be a family birth; of a seasonal event, the start of the blackberry harvest; and around both customs will probably evolve. Underpinning all customs is the ancient understanding of the special and sacred nature of the tree and all we owe them.

All of the tree customs listed below are still observed; global customs would fill another book, so I've just included those familiar to me and hope you will add many from your own landscape heritage. Customs proliferate especially at autumn, when we are gathering their fruits, and in the cold and dark times, when we need the reassurance of continuing life around us.

Autumn/Fall

Autumn is conker season; stringing the fruits of the horse chestnut to play conkers.

It is foraging season, with local nut and wild fruit gathering days specific to your area.

Old Michaelmas Day (October 11) is the day to check the oak trees; "If St. Michael brings many acorns, Christmas will cover the fields with snow."

Apple Day (October 21) was instigated thirty years ago to celebrate all things apple. Visit your local orchard and buy from the source.

Samhain/Hallowe'en (October 31), or Punky Night, is the time for tree divination with apple pips and peels, roasting sweet chestnuts, and for apple bobbing.

Guy Fawkes night (November 5) is one of many bonfire traditions that remind us of the tree's value as fuel: fire to heat us through the winter, to purify by burning away the old (garden bonfires), and to bring the dying sun's light safely down to earth into our hearths. There is a bravura, a joyous energy, to lighting a beacon fire as the earth sinks into the time of greatest darkness.

Winter

Tree Dressing Day on the first weekend in December is modern, started by Common Ground in 1990. Its celebration draws on global customs at varying seasons: tying strips of cloth or yarn to a tree—as in clootie trees (see charm 6), tying ribbons around the trunk of the Bodhi tree (Buddhist tradition), tying coloured strings to entreat protection for loved ones (Hindu festival of Raksha Bandhan), and decorating trees with strips of white paper that carry wishes and poems (Japan). These few examples will spark ideas amongst we dryad charmers.

Bringing evergreens inside during the winter is an age-old custom, periodically denounced by the church as Pagan but surviving with great resilience to the present day. Mistletoe is the one evergreen plant that is still banned in some churches.

Christmas tree tradition has spread from Europe far over the globe. Having a tree as the living spirit of green life, lit and shining through winter, answers a deep need in the human psyche, and these days many people are ensuring that they celebrate with a living tree, roots safely potted. Traditionally the Christmas holiday has twelve days of festivities, and there is a prohibition on keeping green decorations up beyond Twelfth Night (modern) or February 2 (mediaeval sources).

Our only complete Druid ritual is the cutting of the mistletoe from the oak [52] six days after the new moon. To kiss beneath it, tradition says pluck one berry per kiss. At any time when you might expect to receive presents, give back to the trees and the wildlife that they support in turn. Develop a habit of passing on the loving thoughts in concrete action toward nature.

The yule log—Good luck came to all who helped drag this in from the forest. Once on the hearth, it was blessed and libated and burned for the whole of the twelve days of Christmas. Traditional woods were oak (England), birch (Scotland), or cherry, sprinkled with wine (France).

Ashen Faggot Night celebrates a different type of yule log in Somerset, UK. In that county, a bundle of ash branches bound with other tree fibres was burnt, and the future was divined from the snap of each willow, hazel, or green ash band holding it, with a toast each time.

At solstice, the elder tree, Frau Holle, gives gifts specifically to women.

Up Helly Aa is a spectacular festival from the Shetlands at the end of January. A full-sized replica of a Viking long ship is dragged in procession to the sea by men with flaming torches, launched, and set on fire with much festivity.

First Footing, from Scotland, on New Year's Eve (Hogmanay), is more important in that country than Christmas. Luck enters the household when a dark-haired stranger is welcomed as the first visitor of the new year, carrying symbolic gifts: coal for warmth, bread for plenty of food, money and greenery for a long life.

Mumming plays—As farm labourers had little work at this time of year, they supplemented their meagre incomes with January activities, one of which was the mumming play, or guising. The common theme is the fight between good and evil (St. George and the Dragon/Turkish Knight), resulting in a death and resurrection by the doctor—the symbolic act of reawakening the earth to life from the death of winter. In modern times, these are sometimes adapted to make that message clearer, substituting Mother Nature for the doctor and trees representing the seasons. The funny, disrespectful

· · · · · · · · · · · ·

52 Complete ritual in appendix 2.

modern references to local events and politicians, rhyming couplets, and absurdities ensure that they are still rambunctious fun in the traditional model.

Wassailing apple and other fruit trees, especially the cider orchards in the southwest of England, have their own ceremony of blessing around January 19. Traditionally held at night, the ceremony involves fire, torches, cider, song, and noise. There are many traditional songs, one of which addresses the trees directly: "Old apple tree, we wassail thee and hope that thou wilt bear..." whilst the singers circled the orchard. The ragged march ends at "Apple Tree Man," the oldest tree, wherein resides the fertility of the orchard. The trees' roots are given a drink of cider from the wassail bowl, and toast is tied to branches, all with noise (sometimes shotguns fired into the air) to scare off evil influences and bless the trees for a good harvest. A bonfire, a play, and convivial drinking and toasting make up the evening.

Spring

Sing for the Trees (March 8) is a modern celebration to raise awareness of the gifts the trees give us. People worldwide are encouraged to join in locally with friends, family, and groups to raise tree-awareness.

Beating the Bounds on Rogation Day (April 25) may hark back to a Roman custom and their god of boundaries, Terminus. Birch and willow—both "whippy" woods—are used for this in a procession round the parish boundaries, beating each boundary stone or marker with the boughs and (if we can believe our early recorded history!) sometimes beating their adolescent carriers to fix the places in their memories whilst the priest beseeches (rogare) for a blessing on the land and the harvest. This dates back to the fifth century and changed from religious to secular ceremony under Elizabeth I, but in some parishes it is still maintained by the clergy in England.

The Easter Egg Tree, or Osterbaum, is a modern custom of German origin gaining popularity in the US. Hanging homemade decorated eggs from branches clumped to make an indoor "tree" is a lovely way to celebrate the renewal of life in the spring and bring nature indoors.

Ash Wednesday, when the palms from Palm Sunday are burnt to mark the congregation's foreheads, was also the day when schoolchildren would carry an ash twig in their sock.

Mayday or Beltane (May 1) is the time when two trees particularly step forward: the birch (as the maypole) and the hawthorn, whose heady scent contributes to a feeling of license, sexuality, and vibrant life after the cold weather. Boughs are gathered to decorate houses but never taken inside, perhaps because of its association with faery, and the maypole and dancers are all decorated with greenery. Children today still gather boughs for "garland day," dance round the maypole and elect a May Queen, with junior schools supporting the tradition. The Green Man is often an addition to modern festivals. The traditional maypoles [53] of Northern Europe—or "summer poles" raised at Midsummer in the Scandinavian countries—come with a swathe of other customs and song, and this green, joyous celebration is perhaps our most visible of tree festivals today.

Oak Apple Day (May 29) in England commemorates the restoration of the English monarchy in 1660. To show their support, people wore sprigs of oak leaves or a sprig with an oak apple on,[54] and in Victorian/Edwardian times children not wearing one could face rough treatment in school. The association with King Charles is the story that, after the battle of Worcester in 1651, he hid in an oak tree to escape capture by the Roundheads.

Summer

St. John's Day Midsummer bonfires (Bonna Night, Ireland) are a reflection of those at the dark of the year. The attachment to St. John the Baptist stems from John's prophecy about the coming of Jesus: "He must increase, but I must decrease," relating to the decreasing hours of sunlight after the solstice. As at Beltane, these bonfires were jumped for luck when they had burnt down.

· · · · · · · · · · · ·

53 First written account is of a birch maypole in Wales in the mid-fourteenth century.

54 An oak apple is a small, round brown gall growing on a twig, produced from the oak apple gall wasp.

Lastly, we feed our urge to get into nature each summer informally with picnics, barbeques, outings, holidays, camps, and festivals. By doing so, we are answering the need to allow our profound connection with nature and the trees to nourish us.

Developing Your Own Customs

New customs arise from these considerations:

❦ Personal: What is important to your life and the life of your family?

❦ Local: What is important in your community and in the landscape at any given time?

These are your starting points, and we honour the ancestral connection by taking guidance from tradition. If you have good reason, then thoughtfully adapt aspects of old customs and bring them into the twenty-first century. Respect them, and always ask the dryads for their blessing.

Respecting the Spirit of the Wild

There are hundreds of individual tree spirits, all with wonderfully rich and resonant names, from areas of ancient European forests. Many countries have a named tutelary deity of their forests. They range from worried old women to genial men, with some definitely challenging spirits in between. Some are horned, some hairy, some accompanied by wolves, some kidnap children or lead travellers from their path...

These cautionary tales keep us safe from the very real dangers of the deep forest, yet that does not mean that these stories are conjured out of nothing. There is an energy in the forest that might not be inimical, but whose potency always has the propensity to be challenging. To call spirits "evil" because we feel nervous in nature is to view them from a human-centric point of view that is not fair or correct—after all, in fairy tales, they also protect children and outcasts.

The point is, tree spirits are not human thinkers; they have a different agenda, and nature is pitiless to those who break her rules. It is not the forest spirit that may kill you when you get lost, but the cumulative effect of being cold, wet, and hungry might. Respect your needs and nature and stay safe. The role of the genius loci is fixed and devoted to their wood, glade, grove, or forest: it will not deviate to save you from your own folly. We, by contrast, are adaptable and can respond to our needs if we use our common sense. With forethought, planning, respect, and this ability, we will get the very most from our experience of the nurturing green world. Go gently, go surely; build your customs and be enriched by them.

Appendix 5

Strategies for Ill Health and Limited Mobility

It has been salutary, living through a global health crisis, to lose our spontaneity—for most of us, the first time this has happened in our adult lives. Every simple journey for essentials has had to comply with our country's restrictions and has involved planning in a way able-bodied people have never had to before.

As one disabled person posted, "Welcome to my world!" And so I am very pleased that contributions from three Druid friends with disabilities, who have found successful strategies to live a life in relationship to the natural world, make up the bulk of this appendix.

My past experience of being unable to walk was mercifully short, though the restricted mobility during my recovery continued for years. I view the attendant feelings of fear, frustration, and tedium through the gentle mists of memory. But I do remember a turning point. This was being well enough to attend a Druid camp and experience starlit nights, campfires, and the ever-present energies of the trees. It was a transformative experience and, in spite of the difficulties of negotiating the uneven ground and sustaining a cracked rib on the first day, I discovered that when coping with physical life was most difficult, nature was the support I most needed.

At times of impaired health, when every instinct is to turn inward and focus on each new symptom, ache, or pain—and of course these do need our attention—a spiritual connection to nature turns our attention outward, to the greater world. Nature is constantly changing, revealing fresh wonders, astonishing us and healing us through connection. An acquaintance who was bedbound for six months after a car accident was ceremonially carried out to a sun lounger every fine day, wrapped in a blanket, before the family went out to work. Surrounded by everything they needed, and with neighbours to check, the time passed. Later they said that six months in the house would have resulted in severe depression ("It would have driven me mad!"), but being in, and a part of, a living environment was constantly diverting.

For some people, staying in the house is not a choice but essential; not a temporary state but permanent. If you live with severe health issues, I hope that the following first-hand accounts of ways that Druids with disabilities gain from nature, within the house and without, will be helpful to you.

So, over to the experts.

Pia Raveneri, OBOD[55] *Serious Illness Group*

As a member of the OBOD Serious Illness group, I have a lot of practice with connecting to trees when I can't get out into nature due to health issues, and I've written down nine different suggestions here.

WAYS TO CONNECT TO TREE ENERGIES WHEN UNABLE TO GO OUTSIDE TO VISIT TREES

1: Study a species of tree online and make notes about it. Do image searches of the leaves and seeds and trunk and canopy and forests they live in. Find out if they support other life forms or have defences to repel them. Learn how humans use and interact with them. Spending any time researching a tree will introduce you to the gardeners and horticulturalists who have learned how to nurture them, it may introduce you to new folklore, it will introduce you to the people who handle them all the time and know them well, and it will show other aspects of them that you wouldn't necessarily be able to access by interacting with the tree physically. The internet will also draw you into a wider community of people who have been talking about specific trees for a long time, taxonomically, as a species, in the garden, in a

· · · · · · · · · · · ·

55 OBOD: The Order of Bards, Ovates and Druids.
    Website: https://druidry.org.

botanical garden, and will show a bevy of people who have learned to love these trees through their own walks of life.

2: Access your Bardic self and draw the trees you remember from memory or trees you love from photographs. Consider picking a tree a week to study, and practice drawing it. This requires no artistic ability, and all you need is a pen or pencil and some paper, though you can make the drawings elaborate too. This allows you to free your intuitive, creative Awen while connecting to the tree spirit itself. Learning its lines and curves, drawing how it holds space in the world, and getting a sense of how your hand wishes to draw it is a deep form of communion. As you draw, imagine the sound of its leaves rubbing together or the birdsong you might hear; you can even turn on a rain or forest noise generator online to make the experience more meditative and immersive.

3: After a period of time, you should have quite a few drawings of trees. Consider making a board or putting the drawings up in a space or room to create an anchor for a grove. While we have internal groves, an external anchor that focuses on trees you have spent weeks of time with gives you a really effective way to travel to a forest from within your own home. After all, if you've spent weeks with those trees, they become much easier to feel around you; you have drawn their presence into the pages, which means their energy signature is right there with you.

4: Guided forest meditations are common, and you'll often find them on free apps like Insight Timer and sites like YouTube. These are especially useful for disabled or anxious people who often can't go outside for various reasons and are designed to bring the forest to you in your home.

5: If you use any Celtic oracle decks or tarot cards, consider pulling a card for that week to focus on and look at the fauna and flora in the card. You can consider spending time talking to the energies in the card. You might want to enter a meditative state and ask the card and the plants and animals if they have any messages for you. A spider might tell you to be patient. A tree might remind you that all of this is temporary, and that while they are waiting for you physically, they are right there to access energy-wise too.

Consider doing spreads or accessing your Ovate side to commune spiritually with the energies of plant and animal totems.

6: Write stories about favourite trees that you visit. Even if you don't know any stories, you can make some up following your intuition and enlivening your connection to Awen. "Grandmother Sheoak in the bushland stands proud and tall, but she's also bedraggled and looks like she's seen one or two fights. A long time ago, there was a big storm that came to the bushland and the lightning spirits saw her and were determined to push her over. 'That's a sheoak [56] on its own! There's no way she can survive us!' They set themselves upon her as the rain fell all around, but she had been wise and planted her roots so deep into the ground water that though they hurt her full-canopied beauty, she survived them. Later, the animals came from all over and realised that she was even more beautiful for everything she had lived through. The ravens came to nest in her branches, the eagles came to rest and watch for prey, and goannas climbed up her trunk to sun themselves in spring." The stories don't have to be long, and you will find yourself establishing profound connections with real trees through these imaginative exercises. You can even share them with creative groups or other people who also know these trees.

7: If you have family with you or people you can call or chat with, maybe you can communally remember your favourite things about your favourite trees, and talk about what they make you feel like, what seasons they put you in mind of, and how they make you feel. If you have fellow Druid friends you can easily talk to that you've gone to physical events with, consider making a Zoom or group chat where you might talk about what nature aspects you remember most from physical gatherings. Rebuild that sense of place and community from your own home; enjoy the sense of being present together.

8: Consider composing songs or poetry for your favourite trees; they can be real trees you have visited, trees you've seen while meditating, or trees you love as an overall species. If possible, you can also work on dances that make you feel the way the certain trees make you feel. Sing the notes that ring true for them in your heart.

. . . .

56 Sheoak is a classification of ironwoods native to Australia.

9: Apply yourself to Ogham [57] study. Whether you are a beginner or someone advanced, there is always a deeper path you can travel by. Times are tough, yes, but there are opportunities in the darkest moments to learn more truths, and as someone who has never been able to get outside and see trees regularly due to myriad health issues, I promise you, the forest and the trees are right there waiting for you all the time, exactly where you are.

Marian White, Pagan Federation Hospital Visitor

Over the years, my health has deteriorated so much that sometimes I am completely bed bound.

It has only been my connection to nature and ability to close my eyes and journey from my broken body into the wild spaces that has got me through this, meeting the elements, spirits of place connecting to other worlds, worlds in which my pain no longer exists—meeting, conversing, singing, and dancing with the dryads, those tall sentinel beings that occupy the forests.

We have a beautiful little stone circle between two birch trees. I first put it together with stones found during my Druid journey, but Rob and my grandson rebuilt it when Rob first became interested in Druidry, so he became connected to the circle, the earth, spirits of place. We are collecting trees in the garden: we have yew, birch, holly, oak, willow, apple, black thorn, rowan, cherry, and lilac. Rob tends the garden, fortunately, but even on my really bad days he will help me get to the circle to lap up the energy and that valuable connection to the earth. The oaks were planted before I started with OBOD; it was a time many years ago when I started a group that was interested in earthwise living, connecting to the spirits of place. These oaks now tower above me in splendour: we have to keep trimming them or they would take over the whole garden.

Many spiritual organisations are wonderful, but as a disabled person, one can feel they are only for fit people. If you're well and able, you can join in,

57 Ogham is an ancient Irish and British alphabet, with each character ascribed to a letter and a tree. It is easily inscribed on wood or stone as the twenty glyphs each have one to five straight lines in varying positions on a long straight line.

but for those with disabilities, it can feel like you can watch from the sidelines. One gathering was nearly my last because of some things that were said and done, but I realised later that if people realised how they'd upset me by being thoughtless, they would be horrified. Inclusivity is still a long way away, despite everyone's best intentions ...

I know from experience how hard it is to get to various functions, and even though I admire those people who are committed enough to travel across the world to get to events, for some of us, just climbing the front steps into a hall to be physically present is like climbing Everest.

I am so pleased to be a voice for the disabled; it's a step in the right direction. Many blessings.

· · · · · · · · ·

And some spiritual groups are responding to needs with grassroots initiatives led by the people who understand the issues best. Here is our last contributor, who is doing just that.

Lee Tanya, Co-Facilitator of the Grove of Brighid

You asked us about health issues and Druid practice ...

It's something that myself and the co-leader of a Grove feel particularly strongly about: health, age, illness, disability.

The Grove that we facilitate was born out of the need for a Grove that was able to accommodate and include all. We both have health issues that restrict, so we formed the Grove of Brighid. Hearth, home, healing. With our gatherings we alternate between our two homes.

We have members with and without physical challenges, we are pedantic about ensuring all are included, no one is left out and made to feel left out or less worthy, regardless of the body that carries them, which can so often be the case—even if unintentionally.

· · · · · · · · ·

Whatever your physical, mental, financial, and practical circumstances, I wish you all the help you need for a fulfilled inner and outer life, and access to the blessings of nature, the dryads, and the whole inspired world to support you.

Bibliography

The more we know, the greater our understanding and intimacy with nature. That is why your own chosen books on the geology, natural history, and local trees will soon become your most well-used possessions.

Gaining and maintaining a magical stance toward the world is another matter. Delve into nature explorations such as those of Robert MacFarlane, which take a spirito-ecological viewpoint evocative of mysterious connection, and flit between inspirational writings. Below is a selection of the books I dip into regularly and cards I use as meditation aids. All reawaken my own creative approach to nature. As you gradually accrue your select library, some of these books might be of interest.

Relating Practically to Nature & Background Knowledge

Blamires, Steve. *Celtic Tree Mysteries*. St. Paul, MN: Llewellyn, 1997.

Cornell, Joseph B. *Sharing Nature with Children*. Watford: Exley Publications, 1981.

Hageneder, Fred, and Satya Singh. *Tree Yoga*. Forres: Earthdancer, 2007.

Harvey, Graham. *Listening People, Speaking Earth*. London: C. S. Hurst & Co., 1997.

Hitching, Francis. *Earth Magic*. London: Picador, 1977.

Holland, Chris. *I Love My World*. Otterton: Wholeland Press, 2009.

MacLellan, Gordon. *Talking to the Earth*. Chieveley: Capall Bann, 1995.

Matthews, John, ed. *The Druid Source Book*. London: Brockhampton Press, 1998.

Patterson, Barry. *The Art of Conversation with the Genius Loci*. Milverton: Capall Bann, 2005.

Steiner, Rudolf. *The Cycle of the Year as Breathing-Process of the Earth*. Spring Valley, NY: Anthroposophic Press, 1984.

Stowe, John R. *The Findhorn Book of Connecting with Nature*. Forres: Findhorn, 2003.

Vince, Ian. *The Lie of the Land*. London: Pan, 2010.

Walditch, Beatrice. *Listening to the Stones*. Avebury: Heart of Albion, 2014.

Poetry/Art Sources of Inspiration

Bromwich, Rachel, trans. *Dafydd ap Gwilym: A Selection of Poems*. Hammondsworth: Penguin, 1985.

Carmichael, Alexander. Chosen and edited by Adam Bittleston. *The Sun Dances: Prayers and Blessings from the Gaelic*. Edinburgh: Floris Books, 1960.

———. *New Moon of the Seasons*. Edinburgh: Floris Books, 1986.

Goldsworthy, Andy. Introduction by Terry Friedman. *Wood*. London: Viking Publishing, 1996.

Hageneder, Fred. *Yew: A History*. Gloucester: F. Sutton Publishing, 2007.

Harrowven, Jean. *Origins of Rhymes, Songs and Sayings*. Whitstable and Walsall: Pryor Publications, 1998.

King, Angela, and Susan Clifford, eds. *Trees Be Company: An Anthology of Poetry*. Totnes: Green Books, 2001.

Llewellyn-Williams, Hilary. *The Tree Calendar*. Bridgend: Poetry Wales Press,1987.

Lofmark, Carl. *Bards and Heroes*. Felin-fach: Llanerch, 1989.

Matthews, Caitlin. *Celtic Devotional.* New Alresford: Godsfield Press, 1996.

Oliver, Mary. *New and Selected Poems.* New York: Beacon, 1992.

Pennar, Meirion, trans. *Taliesin Poems.* Somerset, UK. Llancrch Enterprises, 1988.

Skelton, Robin, and Margaret Blackwood. *Earth, Air, Fire, Water: Pre-Christian and Pagan Elements in British Songs, Rhymes and Ballads.* London: Arkana, 1990.

Yeats, W. B. *Selected Poetry.* London: Pan Books, 1974.

Tree/Plant Oracle Card Sets

Carr-Gomm, Philip, and Stephanie Carr-Gomm. Illustrated by Will Worthington. *The Druid Plant Oracle.* London: Connections Book Publishing, 2007.

Hageneder, Fred, and Anne Heng. *The Tree Angel Oracle.* Forres: Eaerthdancer, 2006.

Matthews, John. Illustrated by Will Worthington. *The Green Man Tree Oracle.* London: Connections Book Publishing, 2003.

Murray, Liz, and Colin Murray. Illustrated by Vanessa Card. *The Celtic Tree Oracle.* London: Eddison/Sadd, 1988.

Pennick, Nigel, and Nigel Jackson. *The Celtic Oracle.* London: Aquarian Press, 1992.

Spangler, David. Illustrated by Jeremy Berg. *Card Decks of the Sidhe.* Traverse City: Lorian Press, 2016.

To Write to the Author

If you wish to contact the author or would like more information about this book, please write to the author in care of Llewellyn Worldwide and we will forward your request. Both the author and the publisher appreciate hearing from you and learning of your enjoyment of this book and how it has helped you. Llewellyn Worldwide cannot guarantee that every letter written to the author can be answered, but all will be forwarded. Please write to:

Penny Billington
℅ Llewellyn Worldwide
2143 Wooddale Drive
Woodbury, MN 55125–2989

Please enclose a self-addressed stamped envelope for reply
or $1.00 to cover costs. If outside the USA, enclose
an international postal reply coupon.

Many of Llewellyn's authors have websites with additional information and resources. For more information, please visit our website:

WWW.LLEWELLYN.COM

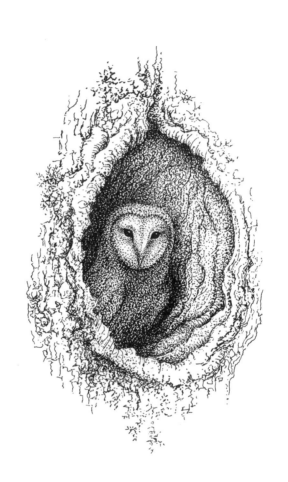